MAN A MACHINE.

MAN A MACHINE

BY

JULIEN OFFRAY DE LA METTRIE

FRENCH-ENGLISH

INCLUDING FREDERICK THE GREAT'S
"EULOGY" ON LA METTRIE AND EX-
TRACTS FROM LA METTRIE'S "THE
NATURAL HISTORY OF THE SOUL"

PHILOSOPHICAL AND HISTORICAL NOTES
BY
GERTRUDE CARMAN BUSSEY
M. A., WELLESLEY COLLEGE

Open Court ● La Salle ● Illinois

TABLE OF CONTENTS.

PREFACE.

THE French text presented in this volume is taken from that of a Leyden edition of 1748, in other words, from that of an edition published in the year and in the place of issue of the first edition. The title page of this edition is reproduced in the present volume. The original was evidently the work of a Dutch compositor unschooled in the French language, and is full of imperfections, inconsistencies, and grammatical blunders By the direction of the publishers these obviously typographical blunders have been corrected by M. Lucien Arréat of Paris.

The translation is the work of several hands. It is founded on a version made by Miss Gertrude C. Bussey (from the French text in the edition of J. Assezat) and has been revised by Professor M. W. Calkins who is responsible for it in its present form. Mademoiselle M. Carret, of the Wellesley College department of French, and Professor George Santayana, of Harvard University, have given valued assistance; and this opportunity is taken to acknowledge their kindness in solving the problems of interpretation which have been submitted to them. It should be added that the translation sometimes subordinates the claims of English structure and style in the effort to render La Mettrie's meaning exactly. The paragraphing of the French is usually followed, but the italics and the capitals are not reproduced. The page-headings of the translation refer back to the pages of the French text; and a few words inserted by the translators are enclosed in brackets.

The philosophical and historical Notes are condensed and adapted from a master's thesis on La Mettrie presented by Miss Bussey to the faculty of Wellesley College.

FREDERIC THE GREAT'S EULOGY ON JULIEN OFFRAY DE LA METTRIE.

FREDERIC THE GREAT'S EULOGY ON JULIEN OFFRAY DE LA METTRIE.

JULIEN Offray de la Mettrie was born in Saint Malo, on the twenty-fifth of December, 1709, to Julien Offray de la Mettrie and Marie Gaudron, who were living by a trade large enough to provide a good education for their son. They sent him to the college of Coutance to study the humanities; he went from there to Paris, to the college of Plessis; he studied his rhetoric at Caen, and since he had much genius and imagination, he won all the prizes for eloquence. He was a born orator, and was passionately fond of poetry and *belles-lettres,* but his father thought that he would earn more as an ecclesiastic than as a poet, and destined him for the church. He sent him, the following year, to the college of Plessis where he studied logic under M. Cordier, who was more a Jansenist than a logician.

It is characteristic of an ardent imagination to seize forcefully the objects presented to it, as it is characteristic of youth to be prejudiced in favor of the first opinions that are inculcated. Any other scholar would have adopted the opinions of his teacher but that was not enough for young La Mettrie; he became a Jansenist, and wrote a work which had great vogue in that party.

In 1725, he studied natural philosophy at the
college of Harcourt, and made great progress there.
On his return to Brittany, M. Hunault, a doctor of
Saint Malo, had advised him to adopt the medical
profession. They had persuaded his father, assuring
him that a mediocre physician would be better paid
for his remedies than a good priest for absolutions.
At first young La Mettrie had applied himself to
the study of anatomy: for two years he had worked
at the dissecting-table. After this, in 1725, he took
the degree of doctor at Rheims, and was there received as a physician.

In 1733, he went to Leyden to study under the famous Boerhaave. The master was worthy of the
scholar and the scholar soon made himself worthy
of the master. M. La Mettrie devoted all the acuteness of his mind to the knowledge and to the heal-
ing of human infirmities; and he soon became a
great physician.

In the year 1734, during his leisure moments, he
translated a treatise of the late M. Boerhaave, his
Aphrodisiacus, and joined to it a dissertation on
venereal maladies, of which he himself was the
author. The old physicians in France rose up
against a scholar who affronted them by knowing
as much as they. One of the most celebrated doctors of Paris did him the honor of criticizing his
work (a sure proof that it was good). La Mettrie
replied; and, to confound his adversary still more,
he composed in 1736 a treatise on vertigo, esteemed
by all impartial physicians.

By an unfortunate effect of human imperfection
a certain base jealousy has come to be one of the
characteristics of men of letters. This feeling incites

those who have reputations, to oppose the progress of budding geniuses. This blight often fastens on talents without destroying them, but it sometimes injures them. M. La Mettrie, who was advancing in the career of science at a giant's pace, suffered from this jealousy, and his quick temper made him too susceptible to it.

In Saint Malo, he translated the "Aphorisms" of Boerhaave, the "Materia Medica," the "Chemical Proceedings," the "Chemical Theory," and the "Institutions," by this same author. About the same time, he published an abstract of Sydenham. The young doctor had learned by premature experience, that if he wished to live in peace, it was better to translate than to compose; but it is characteristic of genius to escape from reflection. Counting on himself alone, if I may speak thus, and filled with the knowledge he had gained from his infinitely skilful researches into nature, he wished to communicate to the public the useful discoveries he had made. He published his treatise on smallpox, his "Practical Medicine," and six volumes of commentary on the physiology of Boerhaave. All these works appeared at Paris, although the author had written them at Saint Malo. He joined to the theory of his art an always successful practice, which is no small recommendation for a physician.

In 1742, La Mettrie came to Paris, led there by the death of M. Hunault, his old teacher. Morand and Sidobre introduced him to the Duke of Gramont, who, a few days after, obtained for him the commission of physician of the guards. He accompanied the Duke to war, and was with him at the battle of Dettingen, at the siege of Freiburg, and at the battle of Fontenoy, where he lost his patron, who was killed by a cannon shot.

La Mettrie felt this loss all the more keenly, because it was at the same time the reef on which his fortune was wrecked. This is what happened. During the campaign of Freiburg, La Mettrie had an attack of violent fever. For a philosopher an illness is a school of physiology; he believed that he could clearly see that thought is but a consequence of the organization of the machine, and that the disturbance of the springs has considerable influence on that part of us which the metaphysicians call soul. Filled with these ideas during his convalescence, he boldly bore the torch of experience into the night of metaphysics; he tried to explain by the aid of anatomy the thin texture of understanding, and he found only mechanism where others had supposed an essence superior to matter. He had his philosophic conjectures printed under the title of "The Natural History of the Soul." The chaplain of the regiment sounded the tocsin against him, and at first sight all the devotees cried out against him.

The common ecclesiastic is like Don Quixote, who found marvelous adventures in commonplace events, or like the famous soldier, so engrossed with his system that he found columns in all the books he read. The majority of priests examine all works of literature as if they were treatises on theology, and filled with this one aim, they discover heresies everywhere. To this fact are due very many false judgments and very many accusations, for the most part unfair, against the authors. A book of physics should be read in the spirit of a physicist; nature, the truth, is its sole judge, and should absolve or condemn it. A book of astronomy should be read in the same manner. If a poor physician proves that the blow of a stick smartly rapped on the skull disturbs the mind, or that at a certain degree of heat reason wanders, one must either prove the contrary or keep quiet. If a skilful astronomer proves, in spite of Joshua, that the earth and all the celestial globes revolve around the sun, one must either calculate better than he, or admit that the earth revolves.

But the theologians, who, by their continual apprehension, might make the weak believe that their cause is bad, are not troubled by such a small matter. They insisted on finding seeds of heresy in a work dealing with physics. The author underwent a frightful persecution, and the priests claimed that a doctor accused of heresy could not cure the French guards.

To the hatred of the devotees was joined that of his rivals for glory. This was rekindled by a work of La Mettrie's entitled "The Politics of Physicians." A man full of cunning, and carried away by ambition, aspired to the place, then vacant, of first physician to the king of France. He thought that he could gain it by heaping ridicule upon those of his contemporaries who might lay claim to this position. He wrote a libel against them, and abusing the easy friendship of La Mettrie, he enticed him to lend to it the volubility of his pen, and the richness of his imagination. Nothing more was needed to complete the downfall of a man little known, against whom were all appearances, and whose only protection was his merit.

For having been too sincere as a philosopher and

too obliging as a friend, La Mettrie was compelled
to leave his country. The Duke of Duras and the
Viscount of Chaila advised him to flee from the
hatred of the priests and the revenge of the physicians. Therefore, in 1746, he left the hospitals of
the army where he had been placed by M. Sechelles,
and came to Leyden to philosophize in peace. He
there composed his "Penelope," a polemical work
against the physicians in which, after the fashion
of Democritus, he made fun of the vanity of his
profession. The curious result was that the doctors
themselves, though their quackery was painted in
true colors, could not help laughing when they read
it, and that is a sure sign that they had found more
wit than malice in it.

M. La Mettrie after losing sight of his hospitals
and his patients, gave himself up completely to specu-
lative philosophy; he wrote his "Man a Machine"
or rather he put on paper some vigorous thoughts
about materialism, which he doubtless planned to
rewrite. This work, which was bound to displease
men who by their position are declared enemies of
the progress of human reason, roused all the priests
of Leyden against its author. Calvinists, Catholics
and Lutherans forgot for the time that consubstan-
tiation, free will, mass for the dead, and the infalli-
bility of the pope divided them: they all united again
to persecute a philosopher who had the additional
misfortune of being French, at a time when that
monarchy was waging a successful war against their
High Powers.

The title of philosopher and the reputation of
being unfortunate were enough to procure for La
Mettrie a refuge in Prussia with a pension from

the king. He came to Berlin in the month of February in the year 1748; he was there received as a member of the Royal Academy of Science. Medicine reclaimed him from metaphysics, and he wrote a treatise on dysentery, another on asthma, the best that had then been written on these cruel diseases. He sketched works on certain philosophical subjects which he had proposed to look into. By a sequence of accidents which befell him these works were stolen, but he demanded their suppression as soon as they appeared.

La Mettrie died in the house of Milord Tirconnel, minister plenipotentiary of France, whose life he had saved. It seems that the disease, knowing with whom it had to deal, was clever enough to attack his brain first, so that it would more surely confound him. He had a burning fever and was violently delirious. The invalid was obliged to depend upon the science of his colleagues, and he did not find there the resources which he had so often found in his own, both for himself and for the public.

He died on the eleventh of November, 1751, at the age of forty-three years. He had married Louise Charlotte Dréano, by whom he left only a daughter, five years and a few months old.

La Mettrie was born with a fund of natural and inexhaustible gaiety; he had a quick mind, and such a fertile imagination that it made flowers grow in the field of medicine. Nature had made him an orator and a philosopher; but a yet more precious gift which he received from her, was a pure soul and an obliging heart. All those who are not imposed upon by the pious insults of the theologians mourn in La Mettrie a good man and a wise physician.

L'HOMME

MACHINE.

Eſt-ce là ce Raion de l'Eſſence ſuprème,
Que l'on nous peint ſi lumineux?
Eſt-ce là cet Eſprit ſurvivant à nous même?
Il naît avec nos ſens, croit, s'affoiblit
comme eux.
Helas! il périra de même.
VOLTAIRE.

À LEYDE,
De l'Imp. d'ELIE LUZAC, Fils.
MDCCXLVIII.

L'HOMME MACHINE.

IL ne suffit pas à un sage d'étudier la nature et la vérité; il doit oser la dire en faveur du petit nombre de ceux qui veulent et peuvent penser; car pour les autres, qui sont volontairement esclaves des préjugés, il ne leur est pas plus possible d'atteindre la vérité, qu'aux grenouilles de voler.

Je réduis à deux les systèmes des philosophes sur l'âme de l'homme. Le premier, et le plus ancien, est le système du matérialisme; le second est celui du spiritualisme.

Les métaphysiciens qui ont insinué que la matière pourrait bien avoir la faculté de penser, n'ont pas déshonoré leur raison. Pourquoi? C'est qu'ils ont cet avantage (car ici c'en est un) de s'être mal exprimés. En effet, demander si la matière peut penser, sans la considérer autrement qu'en elle-même, c'est demander si la matière peut marquer les heures. On voit d'avance que nous éviterons cet écueil, où Mr. Locke a eu le malheur d'échouer.

Les Leibniziens, avec leurs *monades*, ont élevé une hypothèse inintelligible. Ils ont plutôt spiritualisé la matière, que matérialisé l'âme. Comment peut-on définir un être dont la nature nous est absolument inconnue?

Descartes, et tous les Cartésiens, parmi lesquels il y a longtemps qu'on a compté les Malebranchistes,

ont fait la même faute. Ils ont admis deux substances distinctes dans l'homme, comme s'ils les
avaient vues et bien comptées.

Les plus sages ont dit que l'âme ne pouvait se
connaître que par les seules lumières de la Foi:
cependant, en qualité d'êtres raisonnables, ils ont cru
pouvoir se réserver le droit d'examiner ce que l'Ecri-
ture a voulu dire par le mot *Esprit,* dont elle se sert
en parlant de l'âme humaine; et dans leurs recherches, s'ils ne sont pas d'accord sur ce point avec
les théologiens, ceux-ci le sont-ils davantage entr'eux sur tous les autres?

Voici en peu de mots le résultat de toutes leurs
réflexions.

S'il y a un Dieu, il est auteur de la Nature,
comme de la Révélation; il nous a donné l'une,
pour expliquer l'autre; et la Raison, pour les accor-
der ensemble.

Se défier des connaissances qu'on peut puiser dans
les corps animés, c'est regarder la Nature et la
Révélation comme deux contraires qui se détrui-
sent; et par conséquent, c'est oser soutenir cette absurdité: que Dieu se contredit dans ses divers ouvrages, et nous trompe.

S'il y a une Révélation, elle ne peut donc démentir
la Nature. Par la Nature seule, on peut découvrir
le sens des paroles de l'Evangile, dont l'expérience
seule est la véritable interprète. En effet, les autres
commentateurs jusqu'ici n'ont fait qu'embrouiller
la vérité. Nous allons en juger par l'auteur du
Spectacle de la Nature. "Il est étonnant, dit-il (au
"sujet de Mr. Locke), qu'un homme qui dégrade
"notre âme jusqu'à la croire une âme de boue, ose
"établir la Raison pour juge et souverain arbitre

"des mystères de la Foi ; car, ajoute-t-il, quelle idée
"étonnante aurait-on du Christianisme, si l'on vou-
"lait suivre la Raison ?"

Outre que ces réflexions n'éclaircissent rien par
rapport à la Foi, elles forment de si frivoles objections contre la méthode de ceux qui croient pouvoir interpréter les Livres Saints, que j'ai presque
honte de perdre le temps à les réfuter.

1º. L'excellence de la Raison ne dépend pas d'un
grand mot vide de sens (*l'immatérialité*) ; mais de
sa force, de son étendue, ou de sa clairvoyance.
Ainsi une *âme de boue,* qui découvrirait, comme
d'un coup d'œil, les rapports et les suites d'une infinité d'idées difficiles à saisir, serait évidemment
préférable à une âme sotte et stupide qui serait
faite des éléments les plus précieux. Ce n'est pas
être philosophe, que de rougir avec Pline de la
misère de notre origine. Ce qui parait vil, est ici la
chose la plus précieuse, et pour laquelle la nature
semble avoir mis le plus d'art et le plus d'appareil.
Mais comme l'homme, quand même il viendrait
d'une source encore plus vile en apparence, n'en
serait pas moins le plus parfait de tous les êtres,
quelle que soit l'origine de son âme, si elle est pure,
noble, sublime, c'est une belle âme, qui rend respectable quiconque en est doué.

La seconde manière de raisonner de Mr. Pluche
me parait vicieuse, même dans son système, qui tient
un peu du fanatisme ; car si nous avons une idée
de la Foi, qui soit contraire aux principes les plus
clairs, aux vérités les plus incontestables, il faut
croire, pour l'honneur de la Révélation et de son
Auteur, que cette idée est fausse, et que nous ne

connaissons point encore les sens des paroles de l'Evangile.

De deux choses l'une; ou tout est illusion, tant la Nature même, que la Révélation; ou l'expérience seule peut rendre raison de la Foi. Mais quel plus grand ridicule que celui de notre auteur? Je m'imagine entendre un péripatéticien, qui dirait: "Il ne faut "pas croire l'expérience de Toricelli: car si nous la "croyions, si nous allions bannir l'horreur du vide, "quelle étonnante philosophie aurions-nous?"

J'ai fait voir combien le raisonnement de Mr. Pluche est vicieux,* afin de prouver premièrement que s'il y a une Révélation, elle n'est point suffisamment démontrée par la seule autorité de l'Eglise et sans aucun examen de la Raison, comme le prétendent tous ceux qui la craignent. Secondement, pour mettre à l'abri de toute attaque la méthode de ceux qui voudraient suivre la voie que je leur ouvre, d'interpréter les choses surnaturelles, incompréhensibles en soi, par les lumières que chacun a reçues de la nature.

L'expérience et l'observation doivent donc seules nous guider ici. Elles se trouvent sans nombre dans les Fastes des médecins, qui ont été philosophes, et non dans les philosophes, qui n'ont pas été médecins. Ceux-ci ont parcouru, ont éclairé le labyrinthe de l'homme; ils nous ont seuls dévoilé ces ressorts cachés sous des enveloppes qui dérobent à nos yeux tant de merveilles. Eux seuls, contemplant tranquillement notre âme, l'ont mille fois surprise, et dans sa misère, et dans sa grandeur, sans plus la mépriser dans l'un de ces états, que l'admirer dans l'autre. Encore une fois, voilà les seuls physiciens

* Il pèche evidemment par une pétition de principe.

qui aient droit de parler ici. Que nous diraient les autres, et surtout les théologiens? N'est-il pas ridicule de les entendre décider sans pudeur, sur un sujet qu'ils n'ont point été à portée de connaître, dont ils ont été au contraire entièrement détournés par des études obscures, qui les ont conduits à mille préjugés, et pour tout dire en un mot, au fanatisme, qui ajoute encore à leur ignorance dans le mécanisme des corps.

Mais, quoique nous ayons choisi les meilleurs guides, nous trouverons encore beaucoup d'épines et d'obstacles dans cette carrière.

L'homme est une machine si composée, qu'il est impossible de s'en faire d'abord une idée claire, et conséquemment de la définir. C'est pourquoi toutes les recherches que les plus grands philosophes ont faites à *priori*, c'est à dire, en voulant se servir en quelque sorte des aîles de l'esprit, ont été vaines. Ainsi ce n'est qu'à *posteriori*, ou en cherchant à demêler l'âme comme au travers les organes du corps, qu'on peut, je ne dis pas découvrir avec évidence la nature même de l'homme, mais atteindre le plus grand degré de probabilité possible sur ce sujet.

Prenons donc le bâton de l'expérience, et laissons là l'histoire de toutes les vaines opinions des philosophes. Etre aveugle, et croire pouvoir se passer de ce bâton, c'est le comble de l'aveuglement. Qu'un moderne a bien raison de dire qu'il n'y a que la vanité seule qui ne tire pas des causes secondes le même parti que des premières! On peut et on doit même admirer tous ces beaux génies dans leurs travaux les plus inutiles, les Descartes, les Malebranche, les Leibnitz, les Wolf, etc.; mais quel fruit,

je vous prie, a-t-on retiré de leurs profondes médi-
tations et de tous leurs ouvrages? Commençons
donc et voyons, non ce qu'on a pensé, mais ce qu'il
faut penser pour le repos de la vie.

Autant de tempéraments, autant d'esprits, de ca-
ractères et de mœurs différentes. Galien même a
connu cette vérité, que Descartes, et non Hippocrate,
comme le dit l'auteur de l'histoire de l'Ame, a pous-
sée loin, jusqu'à dire que la médecine seule pouvait
changer les esprits et les mœurs avec le corps. Il
est vrai, la mélancolie, la bile, le phlegme, le sang
etc., suivant la nature, l'abondance et la diverse com-
binaison de ces humeurs, de chaque homme font un
homme différent.

Dans les maladies, tantôt l'âme s'éclipse et ne
montre aucun signe d'elle-même; tantôt on dirait
qu'elle est double, tant la fureur la transporte; tantôt l'imbécilité se dissipe: et la convalescence d'un
sot fait un homme d'esprit. Tantôt le plus beau
génie devenu stupide, ne se reconnait plus. Adieu
toutes ces belles connaissances acquises à si grands
frais, et avec tant de peine!

Ici c'est un paralytique, qui demande si sa jambe
est dans son lit: là c'est un soldat qui croit avoir le
bras qu'on lui a coupé. La mémoire de ses anciennes sensations, et du lieu où son âme les rap-
portait, fait son illusion et son espèce de délire.
Il suffit de lui parler de cette partie qui lui manque,
pour lui en rappeller et faire sentir tous les mouvements; ce qui se fait avec je ne sais quel déplaisir
d'imagination qu'on ne peut exprimer.

Celui-ci pleure, comme un enfant, aux approches
de la mort, que celui-là badine. Que fallait-il à
Caius Julius, à Sénèque, à Pétrone pour changer

leur intrépidité en pusillanimité ou en poltronnerie?
Une obstruction dans la rate, dans le foie, un embarras dans la veine porte. Pourquoi? Parceque
l'imagination se bouche avec les viscères; et de là
naissent tous ces singuliers phénomènes de l'affection hystérique et hypocondriaque.

Que dirais-je de nouveau sur ceux qui s'imaginent
être transformés en *loups-garous,* en *coqs,* en *vam-*
pires, qui croient que les morts les sucent? Pourquoi m'arrêterais-je à ceux qui voient leur nez, ou
autres membres, de verre, et à qui il faut conseiller
de coucher sur la paille, de peur qu'ils ne se cassent,
afin qu'ils en retrouvent l'usage et la véritable chair,
lorsque mettant le feu à la paille on leur fait craindre
d'être brûlés: frayeur qui a quelquefois guéri la
paralysie? Je dois légèrement passer sur des choses
connues de tout le monde.

Je ne serai pas plus long sur le détail des effets
du sommeil. Voyez ce soldat fatigué! il ronfle dans
la tranchée, au bruit de cent pièces de canons! Son
âme n'entend rien, son sommeil est une parfaite
apoplexie. Une bombe va l'écraser; il sentira peut-
être moins ce coup qu'un insecte qui se trouve sous
le pied.

D'un autre côté, cet homme que la jalousie, la
haine, l'avarice ou l'ambition dévore, ne peut
trouver aucun repos. Le lieu le plus tranquille, les
boissons les plus fraîches et les plus calmantes, tout
est inutile à qui n'a pas délivré son cœur du tour-
ment des passions.

L'âme et le corps s'endorment ensemble. A
mesure que le mouvement du sang se calme, un
doux sentiment de paix et de tranquillité se répand
dans toute la machine; l'âme se sent mollement

s'appesantir avec les paupières et s'affaisser avec les fibres du cerveau : elle devient ainsi peu à peu comme paralytique, avec tous les muscles du corps. Ceux-ci ne peuvent plus porter le poids de la tête ; celle là ne peut plus soutenir le fardeau de la pensée ; elle est dans le sommeil, comme n'étant point.

La circulation se fait-elle avec trop de vitesse ? l'âme ne peut dormir. L'âme est-elle trop agitée, le sang ne peut se calmer ; il galope dans les veines avec un bruit qu'on entend : telles sont les deux causes réciproques de l'insomnie. Une seule frayeur dans les songes fait battre le cœur à coups redoublés, et nous arrache à la nécessité, ou à la douceur du repos, comme feraient une vive douleur ou des besoins urgents. Enfin, comme la seule cessation des fonctions de l'âme procure le sommeil, il est, même pendant la veille (qui n'est alors qu'une demiveille), des sortes de petits sommeils d'âme très fréquents, des *rêves à la Suisse,* qui prouvent que l'âme n'attend pas toujours le corps pour dormir ; car si elle ne dort pas tout-à-fait, combien peu s'en faut-il ! puisqu'il lui est impossible d'assigner un seul objet auquel elle ait prêté quelque attention, parmi cette foule innombrable d'idées confuses, qui comme autant de nuages remplissent, pour ainsi dire, l'atmosphère de notre cerveau.

L'opium a trop de rapport avec le sommeil qu'il procure, pour ne pas le placer ici. Ce remède enivre, ainsi que le vin, le café, et chacun à sa manière, et suivant sa dose. Il rend l'homme heureux dans un état qui semblerait devoir être le tombeau du sentiment, comme il est l'image de la mort. Quelle douce léthargie ! L'âme n'en voudrait jamais sortir. Elle était en proie aux plus grandes douleurs; elle ne sent plus que le seul plaisir de ne plus suffrir et de jouir de la plus charmante tranquillité. L'opium change jusqu'à la volonté; il force l'âme qui voulait veiller et se divertir, d'aller se mettre au lit malgré elle. Je passe sous silence l'histoire des poisons.

C'est en fouettant l'imagination, que le café, cet antidote du vin, dissipe nos maux de tête et nos chagrins, sans nous en ménager, comme cette liqueur, pour le lendemain.

Contemplons l'âme dans ses autres besoins.

Le corps humain est une machine qui monte elle-même ses ressorts; vivante image du mouvement perpétuel. Les aliments entretiennent ce que la fièvre excite. Sans eux l'âme languit, entre en fureur et meurt abattue. C'est une bougie dont la lumière se ranime, au moment de s'éteindre. Mais nourrissez le corps, versez dans ses tuyaux des sucs vigoureux, des liqueurs fortes; alors l'âme généreuse comme elles s'arme d'un fier courage et le soldat que l'eau eut fait fuir, devenu féroce, court gaiement à la mort au bruit des tambours. C'est ainsi que l'eau chaude agite un sang que l'eau froide eut calmé.

Quelle puissance d'un repas! La joie renaît dans un cœur triste; elle passe dans l'âme des convives qui l'expriment par d'aimables chansons, où les Français excellent. Le mélancolique seul est accablé, et l'homme d'étude n'y est plus propre.

La viande crue rend les animaux féroces; les hommes le deviendraient par la même nourriture; cela est si vrai, que la nation anglaise, qui ne mange pas la chair si cuite que nous, mais rouge et sanglante, parait participer de cette férocité plus ou

moins grande, qui vient en partie de tels aliments,
et d'autres causes, que l'éducation peut seule rendre
impuissantes. Cette férocité produit dans l'âme l'orgueil, la haine, le mépris des autres nations, l'in-
docilité et autres sentiments, qui dépravent le caractère, comme des aliments grossiers font un esprit
lourd, épais, dont la paresse et l'indolence sont les
attributs favoris.

Mr. Pope a bien connu tout l'empire de la gour-
mandise, lorsqu'il dit: "Le grave Catius parle tou-
"jours de vertu, et croit que, qui souffre les vicieux
"est vicieux lui-même. Ces beaux sentiments durent
"jusqu'à l'heure du diner; alors il préfère un scélé-
"rat, qui a une table délicate, à un saint frugal.

"Considérez, dit-il ailleurs, le même homme en
"santé, ou en maladie; possédant une belle charge,
"ou l'ayant perdue; vous le verrez chérir la vie, ou
"la détester, fou à la chasse, ivrogne dans une as-
"semblée de province, poli au bal, bon ami en ville,
"sans foi à la cour."

Nous avons eu en Suisse un bailli, nommé Stei-
guer de Wittighofen; il était à jeûn le plus in-
tègre et même le plus indulgent des juges; mais
malheur au misérable qui se trouvait sur la sellette,
lorsqu'il avait fait un grand diner! Il était homme
à faire pendre l'innocent, comme le coupable.

Nous pensons, et même nous ne sommes honnêtes gens, que comme nous sommes gais, ou braves;
tout dépend de la manière dont notre machine est
montée. On dirait en certains moments que l'âme
habite dans l'estomac, et que Van Helmont, en mettant son siège dans le pylore, ne se serait trompé
qu'en prenant la partie pour le tout.

A quels excès la faim cruelle peut nous porter!

Plus de respect pour les entrailles auxquelles on doit ou on a donné la vie; on les déchire à belles dents, on s'en fait d'horribles festins; et dans la fureur dont on est transporté, le plus faible est toujours la proie du plus fort.

La grossesse, cette émule désirée des pâles couleurs, ne se contente pas d'amener le plus souvent à sa suite les goûts dépravés qui accompagnent ces deux états : elle a quelquefois fait exécuter à l'âme les plus affreux complots; effets d'une manie subite, qui étouffe jusqu'à la loi naturelle. C'est ainsi que le cerveau, cette matrice de l'esprit, se pervertit à sa manière, avec celle du corps.

Quelle autre fureur d'homme ou de femme, dans ceux que la continence et la santé poursuivent! C'est peu pour cette fille timide et modeste d'avoir perdu toute honte et toute pudeur; elle ne regarde plus l'inceste, que comme une femme galante regarde l'adultère. Si ses besoins ne trouvent pas de prompts soulagements, ils ne se borneront point aux simples accidents d'une passion utérine, à la manie, etc. ; cette malheureuse mourra d'un mal, dont il y a tant de médecins.

Il ne faut que des yeux pour voir l'influence nécessaire de l'âge sur la raison. L'âme suit les progrès du corps, comme ceux de l'éducation. Dans le beau sexe, l'âme suit encore la délicatesse du tempérament : de là cette tendresse, cette affection, ces sentiments vifs, plutôt fondés sur la passion que sur la raison, ces préjugés, ces superstitions, dont la forte empreinte peut à peine s'effacer, etc. L'homme, au contraire, dont le cerveau et les nerfs participent de la fermeté de tous les solides, a l'esprit, ainsi que les traits du visage, plus nerveux :

l'éducation, dont manquent les femmes, ajoute encore de nouveaux degrés de force à son âme. Avec de tels secours de la nature et de l'art, comment ne serait-il pas plus reconnaissant, plus généreux, plus constant en amitié, plus ferme dans l'adversité? etc. Mais, suivant à peu près la pensée de l'auteur des Lettres sur les Physionomies, qui joint les grâces de l'esprit et du corps à presque tous les sentiments du cœur les plus tendres et les plus délicats ne doit point nous envier une double force, qui ne semble avoir été donnée à l'homme, l'une, que pour se mieux pénétrer des attraits de la beauté, l'autre, que pour mieux servir à ses plaisirs.

Il n'est pas plus nécessaire d'être aussi grand physionomiste que cet auteur pour deviner la qualité de l'esprit par la figure ou la forme des traits, lorsqu'ils sont marqués jusqu'à un certain point, qu'il ne l'est d'être grand médecin pour connaître un mal accompagné de tous ses symptomes évidents. Examinez les portraits de Locke, de Steele, de Boerhaave, de Maupertuis, etc. vous ne serez point surpris de leur trouver des physionomies fortes, des yeux d'aigle. Parcourez-en une infinité d'autres, vous distinguerez toujours le beau du grand génie, et même souvent l'honnête homme du fripon. On a remarqué, par exemple, qu'un poète célèbre réunit (dans son portrait) l'air d'un filou, avec le feu de Prométhée.

L'histoire nous offre un mémorable exemple de la puissance de l'air. Le fameux Duc de Guise était si fort convaincu que Henri III. qui l'avait eu tant de fois en son pouvoir, n'oserait jamais l'assassiner, qu'il partit pour Blois. Le chancelier Chyverni apprenant son départ, s'écria: *voilà un homme perdu!*

Lorsque sa fatale prédiction fut justifiée par l'événement, on lui en demanda la raison. *Il y a vingt ans, dit-il, que je connais le Roi; il est naturellement bon et même faible; mais j'ai observé qu'un rien l'impatiente et le met en fureur, lorsqu'il fait froid.*

Tel peuple a l'esprit lourd et stupide; tel autre l'a vif, léger, pénétrant. D'où cela vient-il, si ce n'est en partie, et de la nourriture qu'il prend, et de la semence de ses pères,* et de ce chaos de divers éléments qui nagent dans l'immensité de l'air? L'esprit a, comme le corps, ses maladies épidémiques et son scorbut.

Tel est l'empire du climat, qu'un homme qui en change se ressent malgré lui de ce changement. C'est une plante ambulante, qui s'est elle-même transplantée; si le climat n'est plus le même, il est juste qu'elle dégénère, ou s'améliore.

On prend tout encore de ceux avec qui l'on vit, leurs gestes, leurs accents, etc., comme la paupière se baisse à la menace du coup dont on est prévenu, ou par la même raison que le corps du spectateur imite machinalement, et malgré lui, tous les mouvements d'un bon pantomime.

Ce que je viens de dire prouve que la meilleure compagnie pour un homme d'esprit, est la sienne, s'il n'en trouve une semblable. L'esprit se rouille avec ceux qui n'en ont point, faute d'être exercé: à la paume, on renvoie mal la balle à qui la sert mal. J'aimerais mieux un homme intelligent, qui n'aurait eu aucune éducation, que s'il en eût eu une mauvaise, pourvu qu'il fût encore assez jeune. Un

---

* L'histoire des animaux et des hommes prouve l'empire de la semence des pères sur l'esprit et le corps des enfants.

esprit mal conduit est un acteur que la province a gâté.

Les divers états de l'âme sont donc toujours corrélatifs à ceux du corps. Mais, pour mieux démontrer toute cette dépendance et ses causes, servons-nous ici de l'anatomie comparée; ouvrons les entrailles de l'homme et des animaux. Le moyen de connaître la nature humaine, si l'on n'est éclairé par un juste parallèle de la structure des uns et des autres!

En général, la forme et la composition du cerveau des quadrupèdes est à peu près la même que dans l'homme. Même figure, même disposition partout; avec cette différence essentielle, que l'homme est de tous les animaux celui qui a le plus de cerveau, et le cerveau le plus tortueux, en raison de la masse de son corps. Ensuite le singe, le castor, l'éléphant, le chien, le renard, le chat, etc., voilà les animaux qui ressemblent le plus à l'homme; car on remarque aussi chez eux la même analogie graduée, par rapport au corps calleux, dans lequel Lancisi avait établi le siège de l'âme, avant feu Mr. de la Peyronnie, qui cependant a illustré cette opinion par une foule d'expériences.

Après tous les quadrupèdes, ce sont les oiseaux qui ont le plus de cerveau. Les poissons ont la tête grosse; mais elle est vide de sens, comme celle de bien des hommes. Ils n'ont point de corps calleux et fort peu de cerveau, lequel manque aux insectes.

Je ne me répandrai point en un plus long détail des variétés de la nature, ni en conjectures, car les unes et les autres sont infinies, comme on en peut juger en lisant les seuls traités de Willis, *De Cerebro,* et *De Anima Brutorum.*

Je conclûrai seulement ce qui s'en suit clairement de ces incontestables observations : 1o que plus les animaux sont farouches, moins ils ont de cerveau; 2o que ce viscère semble s'agrandir, en quelque sorte, à proportion de leur docilité; 3o qu'il y a ici une singulière condition imposée éternellement par la nature, qui est que plus on gagnera du côté de l'esprit, plus on perdra du côté de l'instinct. Lequel l'emporte, de la perte ou du gain?

Ne croyez pas, au reste, que je veuille prétendre par là que le seul volume du cerveau suffise pour faire juger du degré de docilité des animaux; il faut que la qualité réponde encore à la quantité, et que les solides et les fluides soient dans cet équilibre convenable qui fait la santé.

Si l'imbécile ne manque pas de cerveau, comme on le remarque ordinairement, ce viscère péchera par une mauvaise consistance, par trop de mollesse, par exemple. Il en est de même des fous; les vices de leur cerveau ne se dérobent pas toujours à nos recherches; mais si les causes de l'imbécilité, de la folie, etc. ne sont pas sensibles, où aller chercher celles de la variété de tous les esprits? Elles échapperaient aux yeux des lynx et des argus. *Un rien, une petite fibre, quelque chose que la plus subtile anatomie ne peut découvrir,* eut fait deux sots d'Erasme et de Fontenelle, qui le remarque lui même dans un de ses meilleurs *Dialogues.*

Outre la mollesse de la moëlle du cerveau, dans les enfants, dans les petits chiens et dans les oiseaux, Willis a remarqué que les *corps cannelés* sont effacés et comme décolorés dans tous ces animaux, et que leurs *stries* sont aussi imparfaitement formées que dans les paralytiques. Il ajoute, ce qui est vrai, que l'homme a la protubérance annulaire fort grosse; et ensuite toujours diminutivement par dégrés, le singe et les autres animaux nommés ci-devant, tandis que le veau, le bœuf, le loup, la brebis, le cochon, etc. qui ont cette partie d'un très petit volume, ont les *nattes* et *testes* fort gros.

On a beau être discret et réservé sur les conséquences qu'on peut tirer de ces observations et de tant d'autres sur l'espèce d'inconstance des vaisseaux et des nerfs, etc. : tant de variétés ne peuvent être des jeux gratuits de la nature. Elles prouvent du moins la nécessité d'une bonne et abondante organisation, puisque dans tout le règne animal l'âme, se raffermissant avec le corps, acquiert de la sagacité, à mesure qu'il prend des forces.

Arrêtons-nous à contempler la différente docilité des animaux. Sans doute l'analogie la mieux entendue conduit l'esprit à croire que les causes dont nous avons fait mention produisent toute la diversité qui se trouve entr'eux et nous, quoiqu'il faille avouer que notre faible entendement, borné aux observations les plus grossières, ne puisse voir les liens qui règnent entre la cause et les effets. C'est une espèce d'*harmonie* que les philosophes ne connaîtront jamais.

Parmi les animaux, les uns apprennent à parler et à chanter; ils retiennent des airs et prennent tous les tons aussi exactement qu'un musicien. Les autres, qui montrent cependant plus d'esprit, tels que le singe, n'en peuvent venir à bout. Pourquoi cela, si ce n'est par un vice des organes de la parole?

Mais ce vice est-il tellement de conformation,

qu'on n'y puisse apporter aucun remède? en un mot serait-il absolument impossible d'apprendre une langue à cet animal? Je ne le crois pas.

Je prendrais le grand singe préférablement à tout autre, jusqu'à ce que le hasard nous eût fait découvrir quelque autre espèce plus semblable à la nôtre, car rien ne répugne qu'il y en ait dans des régions qui nous sont inconnues. Cet animal nous ressemble si fort, que les naturalistes l'ont appelé *homme sauvage,* ou *homme des bois.* Je le prendrais aux mêmes conditions des écoliers d'Amman; c'est-à-dire, que je voudrais qu'il ne fût ni trop jeune ni trop vieux; car ceux qu'on nous apporte en Europe sont communément trop âgés. Je choisirais celui qui aurait la physionomie la plus spirituelle, et qui tiendrait le mieux dans mille petites opérations ce qu'elle m'aurait promis. Enfin, ne me trouvant pas digne d'être son gouverneur, je le mettrais à l'école de l'excellent maître que je viens de nommer, ou d'un autre aussi habile, s'il en est.

Vous savez par le livre d'Amman, et par tous ceux* qui ont traduit sa méthode, tous les prodiges qu'il a su opérer sur les sourds de naissance, dans les yeux desquels il a, comme il le fait entendre lui-même, trouvé des oreilles; et en combien peu de temps enfin il leur a appris à entendre, parler, lire, et écrire. Je veux que les yeux d'un sourd voient plus clair et soient plus intelligents que s'il ne l'était pas, par la raison que la perte d'un membre ou d'un sens peut augmenter la force ou la pénétration d'un autre: mais le singe voit et entend; il comprend ce qu'il entend et ce qu'il voit; il conçoit si parfaitement les signes qu'on lui fait, qu'à tout autre jeu,

* L'auteur de l'Histoire naturelle de l'âme etc.

ou tout autre exercice, je ne doute point qu'il ne
l'emportât sur les disciples d'Amman. Pourquoi
donc l'éducation des singes serait-elle impossible?
Pourquoi ne pourrait-il enfin, à force de soins, imiter, à l'exemple des sourds, les mouvemens néces-
saires pour prononcer? Je n'ose décider si les organes de la parole du singe ne peuvent, quoiqu'on
fasse, rien articuler; mais cette impossibilité absolue
me surprendrait, à cause de la grande analogie du
singe et de l'homme, et qu'il n'est point d'animal
connu jusqu'à présent, dont le dedans et le dehors
lui ressemblent d'une manière si frappante. Mr.
Locke, qui certainement n'a jamais été suspect de
crédulité, n'a pas fait difficulté de croire l'histoire
que le Chevalier Temple fait dans ses Mémoires,
d'un perroquet qui répondait à propos et avait
appris, comme nous, à avoir une espèce de conversation suivie. Je sais qu'on s'est moqué* de ce grand
métaphysicien; mais qui aurait annoncé à l'univers
qu'il y a des générations qui se font sans œufs et
sans femmes, aurait-il trouvé beaucoup de partisans? Cependant Mr. Trembley en a découvert,
qui se font sans accouplement, et par la seule section. Amman n'eût-il pas aussi passé pour un fou,
s'il se fût vanté, avant que d'en faire l'heureuse expérience, d'instruire, et en aussi peu de temps, des
écoliers tels que les siens? Cependant ses succès
ont étonné l'univers, et comme l'auteur de l'Histoire des Polypes, il a passé de plein vol à l'immortalité. Qui doit à son génie les miracles qu'il opère,
l'emporte à mon gré sur qui doit les siens au hasard. Qui a trouvé l'art d'embellir le plus beau des
règnes, et de lui donner des perfections qu'il n'a-

---

* L'auteur de l'Hist. de l'âme.

vait pas, doit être mis au-dessus d'un faiseur oisif de systèmes frivoles, ou d'un auteur laborieux de stériles découvertes. Celles d'Amman sont bien d'un autre prix; il a tiré les hommes de l'instinct auquel ils semblaient condamnés; il leur a donné les idées, de l'esprit, une âme en un mot, qu'ils n'eûssent jamais eue. Quel plus grand pouvoir!

Ne bornons point les ressources de la nature; elles sont infinies, surtout aidées d'un grand art.

La même mécanique, qui ouvre le canal d'Eustachi dans les sourds, ne pourrait-il le déboucher dans les singes? Une heureuse envie d'imiter la prononciation du maître, ne pourrait-elle mettre en liberté les organes de la parole, dans les animaux qui imitent tant d'autres signes, avec tant d'adresse et d'intelligence? Non seulement je défie qu'on me cite aucune expérience vraiment concluante, qui décide mon projet impossible et ridicule; mais la similitude de la structure et des opérations du singe est telle, que je ne doute presque point, si on exerçait parfaitement cet animal, qu'on ne vînt enfin à bout de lui apprendre à prononcer, et par conséquent à savoir une langue. Alors ce ne serait plus ni un homme sauvage, ni un homme manqué: ce serait un homme parfait, un petit homme de ville, avec autant d'étoffe ou de muscles que nous-mêmes, pour penser et profiter de son éducation.

Des animaux à l'homme, la transition n'est pas violente; les vrais philosophes en conviendront. Qu'était l'homme, avant l'invention des mots et la connaissance des langues? Un animal de son espèce, qui avec beaucoup moins d'instinct naturel que les autres, dont alors il ne se croyait pas roi, n'était distingué du singe et des autres animaux

que comme le singe l'est lui-même; je veux dire par
une physionomie qui annonçait plus de discerne-
ment. Réduit à la seule *connaissance intuitive* des
Leibniziens, il ne voyait que des figures et des couleurs, sans pouvoir rien distinguer entr'elles; vieux,
comme jeune, enfant à tout âge, il bégayait ses sensations et ses besoins, comme un chien affamé, ou
ennuyé de repos, demande à manger ou à se pro-
mener.

Les mots, les langues, les lois, les sciences, les
beaux-arts sont venus; et par eux enfin le diamant
brut de notre esprit a été poli. On a dressé un
homme, comme un animal; on est devenu auteur,
comme portefaix. Un géomètre a appris à faire
les démonstrations et les calculs les plus difficiles,
comme un singe à ôter ou mettre son petit chapeau,
et à monter sur son chien docile. Tout s'est fait
par les signes; chaque espèce a compris ce qu'elle
a pu comprendre: et c'est de cette manière que les
hommes ont acquis *la connaissance symbolique,* ainsi
nommée encore par nos philosophes d'Allemagne.

Rien de si simple, comme on voit, que la mécanique de notre éducation! Tout se réduit à des
sons, ou à des mots, qui de la bouche de l'un passent
par l'oreille de l'autre dans le cerveau, qui reçoit
en même temps par les yeux la figure des corps, dont
ces mots sont les signes arbitraires.

Mais qui a parlé le premier? Qui a été le premier précepteur du genre human? Qui a inventé
les moyens de mettre à profit la docilité de notre
organisation? Je n'en sais rien; le nom de ces heureux et premiers génies a été perdu dans la nuit
des temps. Mais l'art est le fils de la nature; elle
a dû longtemps le précéder.

On doit croire que les hommes les mieux organisés, ceux pour qui la nature aura épuisé ses bienfaits, auront instruit les autres. Ils n'auront pu
entendre un bruit nouveau, par exemple, éprouver de
nouvelles sensations, être frappé de tous ces beaux
objets divers qui forment le ravissant spectacle de
la nature, sans se trouver dans le cas de ce sourd
de Chartres dont le grand Fontenelle nous a le
premier donné l'histoire, lorsqu'il entendit pour la
première fois à quarante ans le bruit étonnant des
cloches.

De là serait-il absurde de croire que ces premiers
mortels essayèrent à la manière de ce sourd, ou à
celle des animaux et des muets (autre espèce
d'animaux), d'exprimer leurs nouveaux sentiments
par des mouvements dépendants de l'économie de
leur imagination, et conséquemment ensuite par des
sons spontanés propres à chaque animal, expression
naturelle de leur surprise, de leur joie, de leurs
transports, ou de leurs besoins? Car sans doute
ceux que la nature a doués d'un sentiment plus
exquis, ont eu aussi plus de facilité pour l'exprimer.

Voilà comme je conçois que les hommes ont employé leur sentiment, ou leur instinct, pour avoir de
l'esprit, et enfin leur esprit, pour avoir des connaissances. Voilà par quels moyens, autant que je puis
les saisir, on s'est rempli le cerveau des idées, pour
le réception desquelles la nature l'avait formé. On
s'est aidé l'un par l'autre; et les plus petits com-
mencements s'agrandissant peu à peu, toutes les
choses de l'univers ont été aussi facilement dis-
tinguées qu'un cercle.

Comme une corde de violon ou une touche de
clavecin frémit et rend un son, les cordes du cer-

veau, frappées par les rayons sonores, ont été ex-
citées à rendre ou à redire les mots qui les tou-
chaient. Mais comme telle est la construction de
ce viscère, que dès qu'une fois les yeux bien formés
pour l'optique ont reçu la peinture des objets, le
cerveau ne peut pas ne pas voir leurs images et leurs
différences : de même, lorsque les signes de ces
différences ont été marqués, ou gravés dans le cerveau, l'âme en a nécessairement examiné les rapports ; examen qui lui était impossible sans la découverte des signes, ou l'invention des langues.
Dans ces temps, où l'univers était presque muet,
l'âme était à l'égard de tous les objets, comme un
homme qui, sans avoir aucune idée des proportions, regarderait un tableau, ou une pièce de sculpture : il n'y pourrait rien distinguer ; ou comme un
petit enfant (car alors l'âme était dans son enfance) qui, tenant dans sa main un certain nombre
de petits brins de paille ou de bois, les voit en général d'une vue vague et superficielle, sans pouvoir
les compter ni les distinguer. Mais qu'on mette
une espèce de pavillon, ou d'étendard, à cette pièce
de bois, par exemple, qu'on appelle mât, qu'on en
mette un autre à un autre pareil corps ; que le premier venu se nombre par le signe 1 et le second
par le signe ou chiffre 2 ; alors cet enfant pourra les
compter, et ainsi de suite il apprendra toute l'arith-
métique. Dès qu'une figure lui paraîtra égale à
une autre par son signe *numératif*, il conclûra sans
peine que ce sont deux corps différents ; que 1 et 1
font deux, que 2 et 2 font 4,* etc.

C'est cette similitude réelle, ou apparente, des

---

*Il y a encore aujourd'hui des peuples, qui, faute d'un plus
grand nombre de signes, ne peuvent compter que jusqu'à 20.

figures, qui est la base fondamentale de toutes les vérités et de toutes nos connaissances, parmi lesquelles il est évident que celles dont les signes sont moins simples et moins sensibles sont plus difficiles à apprendre que les autres, en ce qu'elles demandent plus de génie pour embrasser et combiner cette immense quantité de mots par lesquels les sciences dont je parle expriment les vérités de leur ressort : tandis que les sciences qui s'annoncent par des chiffres, ou autres petits signes, s'apprennent facilement ; et c'est sans doute cette facilité qui a fait la fortune des calculs algébriques, plus encore que leur évidence.

Tout ce savoir dont le vent enfle le ballon du cerveau de nos pédants orgueilleux, n'est donc qu'un vaste amas de mots et de figures, qui forment dans la tête toutes les traces par lesquelles nous distinguons et nous nous rappellons les objets. Toutes nos idées se réveillent, comme un jardinier qui connaît les plantes se souvient de toutes leurs phases à leur aspect. Ces mots et ces figures qui sont désignés par eux, sont tellements liés ensemble dans le cerveau, qu'il est assez rare qu'on imagine une chose sans le nom ou le signe qui lui est attaché.

Je me sers toujours du mot *imaginer,* parceque je crois que tout s'imagine, et que toutes les parties de l'âme peuvent être justement réduites à la seule imagination, qui les forme toutes ; et qu'ainsi le jugement, le raisonnement, la mémoire ne sont que des parties de l'âme nullement absolues, mais de véritables modifications de cette espèce de *toile médullaire,* sur laquelle les objets peints dans l'œil sont renvoyés, comme d'une lanterne magique.

Mais si tel est ce merveilleux et incompréhensible résultat de l'organisation du cerveau; si tout se conçoit par l'imagination, si tout s'explique par elle; pourquoi diviser le principe sensitif qui pense dans l'homme?   N'est-ce pas une contradiction mani-feste dans les partisans de la simplicité de l'esprit? Car une chose qu'on divise ne peut plus être, sans absurdité, regardée comme indivisible.   Voilà où conduit l'abus des langues, et l'usage de ces grands mots, *spiritualité, immatérialité,* etc., placés à tout hasard, sans être entendus, même par des gens d'esprit.

Rien de plus facile que de prouver un système, fondé comme celui-ci sur le sentiment intime et l'ex-périence propre de chaque individu.   L'imagination, ou cette partie fantastique du cerveau, dont la nature nous est aussi inconnue que sa manière d'agir, est-elle naturellement petite, ou faible? elle aura à peine la force de comparer l'analogie, ou la ressemblance de ses idées; elle ne pourra voir que ce qui sera vis-à-vis d'elle, ou ce qui l'affectera le plus vive-ment; et encore de quelle manière! Mais toujours est-il vrai que l'imagination seule aperçoit; que c'est elle qui se représente tous les objets, avec les mots et les figures qui les caractérisent; et qu'ainsi c'est elle encore une fois qui est l'âme, puisqu'elle en fait tous les rôles.   Par elle, par son pinceau flat-teur, le froid squelette de la raison prend des chairs vives et vermeilles; par elle les sciences fleurissent, les arts s'embellissent, les bois parlent, les échos soupirent, les rochers pleurent, le marbre respire, tout prend vie parmi les corps inanimés.   C'est elle encore qui ajoute à la tendresse d'un cœur amoureux le piquant attrait de la volupté; elle la fait ger-

mer dans le cabinet du philosophe, et du pédant
poudreux; elle forme enfin les savants comme les
orateurs et les poëtes. Sottement décriée par les
uns, vainement distinguée par les autres, qui tous
l'ont mal connue, elle ne marche pas seulement à la
suite des Grâces et des beaux-art, elle ne peint pas
seulement la nature, elle peut aussi la mesurer.
Elle raisonne, juge, pénètre, compare, approfondit.
Pourrait-elle si bien sentir les beautées des tableaux
qui lui sont tracés, sans en découvrir les rapports?
Non; comme elle ne peut se replier sur les plaisirs
des sens, sans en goûter toute la perfection ou la
volupté, elle ne peut réfléchir sur ce qu'elle a méca-
niquement conçu, sans être alors le jugement même.

Plus on exerce l'imagination, ou le plus maigre
génie, plus il prend, pour ainsi dire, d'embonpoint;
plus il s'agrandit, devient nerveux, robuste, vaste
et capable de penser. La meilleure organisation a
besoin de cet exercice.

L'organisation est le premier mérite de l'homme;
c'est en vain que tous les auteurs de morale ne
mettent point au rang des qualités estimables celles
qu'on tient de la nature, mais seulement les talents
qui s'acquièrent à force de réflexions et d'industrie:
car d'où nous vient, je vous prie, l'habileté, la science et la vertu, si ce n'est d'une disposition qui
nous rend propres à devenir habiles, savants et vertueux? Et d'où nous vient encore cette disposition,
si ce n'est de la nature? Nous n'avons de qualités
estimables que par elle; nous lui devons tout ce que
nous sommes. Pourquoi donc n'estimerais-je pas
autant ceux qui ont des qualités naturelles, que
ceux qui brillent par des vertus acquises, et comme
d'emprunt? Quel que soit le mérite, de quelque en-

droit qu'il naisse, il est digne d'estime; il ne s'agit
que de savoir le mesurer. L'esprit, la beauté, les
richesses, la noblesse, quoiqu'enfants du hasard,
ont tous leur prix, comme l'adresse, le savoir, la
vertu, etc. Ceux que la nature a comblés de ses dons
les plus précieux, doivent plaindre ceux à qui ils
ont été refusés; mais ils peuvent sentir leur supé-
riorité sans orgueil, et en connaisseurs. Une belle
femme serait aussi ridicule de se trouver laide,
qu'un homme d'esprit de se croire un sot. Une
modestie outrée (défaut rare à la vérité) est une
sorte d'ingratitude envers la nature. Une honnête
fierté, au contraire, est la marque d'une âme belle
et grande, que décèlent des traits mâles moulés
comme par le sentiment.

Si l'organisation est un mérite, et le premier mérite, et la source de tous les autres, l'instruction est
le second. Le cerveau le mieux construit, sans elle,
le serait en pure perte; comme sans l'usage du
monde, l'homme le mieux fait ne serait qu'un pay-
san grossier. Mais aussi quel serait le fruit de la
plus excellente école, sans une matrice parfaitement
ouverte à l'entrée ou à la conception des idées? Il
est aussi impossible de donner une seule idée à un
homme privé de tous les sens, que de faire un
enfant à une femme à laquelle la nature aurait
poussé la distraction jusqu'à oublier de faire une
vulve, comme je l'ai vu dans une, qui n'avait ni
fente, ni vagin, ni matrice, et qui pour cette raison
fut démariée après dix ans de mariage.

Mais si le cerveau est à la fois bien organisé et
bien instruit, c'est une terre féconde parfaitement
ensemencée, qui produit le centuple de ce qu'elle a
reçu: ou (pour quitter le style figuré souvent né-

cessaire, pour mieux exprimer ce qu'on sent et donner des grâces à la Vérité même), l'imagination élevée par l'art à la belle et rare dignité de génie, saisit exactement tous les rapports des idées qu'elle a conçues, embrasse avec facilité une foule étonnante d'objets, pour en tirer enfin une longue chaîne de conséquences, lesquelles ne sont encore que de nouveaux rapports, enfantés par la comparaison des premiers, auxquels l'âme trouve une parfaite ressemblance. Telle est, selon moi, la génération de l'esprit. Je dis *trouve,* comme j'ai donné ci-devant l'épithète *d'apparente* à la similitude des objets: non que je pense que nos sens soient toujours trompeurs, comme l'a prétendu le Père Malebranche, ou que nos yeux naturellement un peu ivres ne voient pas les objets tels qu'ils sont en eux mêmes, quoique les microscopes nous le prouvent tous les jours, mais pour n'avoir aucune dispute avec les Pyrrhoniens, parmi lesquels Bayle s'est distingué.

Je dis de la vérité en général ce que Mr. de Fontenelle dit de certaines en particulier, qu'il faut la sacrifier aus agréments de la société. Il est de la douceur de mon caractère d'obvier à toute dispute, lorsqu'il ne s'agit pas d'aiguiser la conversation. Les Cartésiens viendraient ici vainement à la charge avec leur *idées innées*; je ne me donnerais certainement pas le quart de la peine qu'a prise Mr. Locke pour attaquer de telles chimères. Quelle utilité, en effet, de faire un gros livre, pour prouver une doctrine qui était érigée en axiome il y a trois mille ans?

Suivant les principes que nous avons posés, et que nous croyons vrais, celui qui a le plus d'imagina-

tion doit être regardé comme ayant le plus d'esprit,
ou de génie, car tous ces mots sont synonymes; et
encore une fois c'est par un abus honteux qu'on
croit dire des choses différentes, lorsqu'on ne dit que
différents mots ou différents sons, auxquels on n'a
attaché aucune idée ou distinction réelle.

La plus belle, la plus grande, ou la plus forte
imagination, est donc la plus propre aux sciences,
comme aux arts.   Je ne décide point s'il faut plus
d'esprit pour exceller dans l'art des Aristotes, ou
des Descartes, que dans celui des Euripides ou des
Sophocles; et si la nature s'est mise en plus grands
frais pour faire Newton que pour former Corneille
(ce dont je doute fort), mais il est certain que
c'est la seule imagination diversement appliquée
qui a fait leur différent triomphe et leur gloire immortelle.

Si quelqu'un passe pour avoir peu de jugement,
avec beaucoup d'imagination; cela veut dire que
l'imagination trop abandonnée à elle même, presque
toujours comme occupée à se regarder dans le miroir de ses sensations, n'a pas assez contracté l'habitude de les examiner elles-mêmes avec attention; plus
profondément pénétrée des traces, ou des images,
que de leur vérité ou de leur ressemblance.

Il est vrai que telle est la vivacité des ressorts de
l'imagination, que si l'attention, cette clé ou mère des
sciences, ne s'en mêle, il ne lui est guères permis
que de parcourir et d'effleurer les objets.

Voyez cet oiseau sur la branche, il semble toujours prêt à s'envoler; l'imagination est de même.
Toujours emportée par le tourbillon du sang et des
esprits, une onde fait une trace, effacée par celle
qui suit; l'âme court après, souvent en vain: il faut

qu'elle s'attende à regretter ce qu'elle n'a pas assez vite saisi et fixé : et c'est ainsi que l'imagination, véritable image du temps, se détruit et se renouvelle sans cesse.

Tel est le chaos et la succession continuelle et rapide de nos idées ; elles se chassent, comme un flot pousse l'autre ; de sorte que si l'imagination n'emploie, pour ainsi dire, une partie de ses muscles pour être comme en équilibre sur les cordes du cerveau, pour se soutenir quelque temps sur un objet qui va fuir et s'empêcher de tomber sur un autre, qu'il n'est pas encore temps de contempler, jamais elle ne sera digne du beau nom de jugement. Elle exprimera vivement ce qu'elle aura senti de même ; elle formera des orateurs, des musiciens, des peintres, des poètes, et jamais un seul philosophe. Au contraire si, dès l'enfance, on accoutume l'imagination à se brider elle-même, à ne point se laisser emporter à sa propre impétuosité, qui ne fait que de brillants enthousiastes, à arrêter, contenir ses idées, à les retourner dans tous les sens, pour voir toutes les faces d'un objet, alors l'imagination prompte à juger embrassera par le raisonnement la plus grande sphère d'objets, et sa vivacité, toujours de si bon augure dans les enfants, et qu'il ne s'agit que de régler par l'étude et l'exercice, ne sera plus qu'une pénétration clairvoyante, sans laquelle on fait peu de progrès dans les sciences.

Tels sont les simples fondements sur lesquels a été bati l'édifice de la logique. La nature les avait jetés pour tout le genre humain ; mais les uns en ont profité, les autres en ont abusé.

Malgré toutes ces prérogatives de l'homme sur les animaux, c'est lui faire honneur que de le ran-ger dans la même classe. Il est vrai que, jusqu'à un certain âge, il est plus animal qu'eux, parce qu'il apporte moins d'instinct en naissant.

Quel est l'animal qui mourrait de faim au milieu d'une rivière de lait? L'homme seul. Semblable à ce vieux enfant dont un moderne parle d'après Arnobe, il ne connait ni les aliments qui lui sont propres, ni l'eau qui peut le noyer, ni le feu qui peut le réduire en poudre. Faites briller pour la première fois la lumière d'une bougie aux yeux d'un enfant, il y portera machinalement le doigt, comme pour savoir quel est le nouveau phénomène qu'il aperçoit; c'est à ses dépens qu'il en connaîtra le danger, mais il n'y sera pas repris.

Mettez-le encore avec un animal sur le bord d'un précipice! lui seul y tombera; il se noie, où l'autre se sauve à la nage. A quatorze ou quinze ans, il entrevoit à peine les grands plaisirs qui l'attendent dans la reproduction de son espèce; déjà adolescent, il ne sait pas trop comment s'y prendre dans un jeu que la nature apprend si vite aux animaux: il se cache, comme s'il était honteux d'avoir du plaisir et d'être fait pour être heureux, tandis que les animaux se font gloire d'être *cyniques.* Sans éducation, ils sont sans préjugés. Mais voyons encore ce chien et cet enfant qui ont tous deux perdu leur maître dans un grand chemin: l'enfant pleure, il ne sait à quel saint se vouer; le chien, mieux servi par son odorat que l'autre par sa raison, l'aura bientôt trouvé.

La nature nous avait donc faits pour être au dessous des animaux, ou du moins pour faire par là même mieux éclater les prodiges de l'éducation, qui seule nous tire du niveau et nous élève enfin au-dessus d'eux. Mais accordera-t-on la même distinction aux sourds, aux aveugles-nés, aux imbéciles, aux fous, aux hommes sauvages, ou qui ont été élevés dans les bois avec les bêtes, à ceux dont l'affection hypocondriaque a perdu l'imagination, enfin à toutes ces bêtes à figure humaine, qui ne montrent que l'instinct le plus grossier ? Non, tous ces hommes de corps, et non d'esprit, ne méritent pas une classe particulière.

Nous n'avons pas dessein de nous dissimuler les objections qu'on peut faire en faveur de la distinction primitive de l'homme et des animaux, contre notre sentiment. Il y a, dit-on, dans l'homme une loi naturelle, une connaissance du bien et du mal, qui n'a pas été gravée dans le cœur des animaux.

Mais cette objection, ou plutôt cette assertion est-elle fondée sur l'expérience, sans laquelle un philosophe peut tout rejeter ? En avons-nous quelqu'une qui nous convainque que l'homme seul a été éclairé d'un rayon refusé à tous les autres animaux ? S'il n'y en a point, nous ne pouvons pas plus connaître par elle ce qui se passe dans eux, et même dans les hommes, que ne pas sentir ce qui affecte l'intérieur de notre être. Nous savons que nous pensons et que nous avons des remords : un sentiment intime ne nous force que trop d'en convenir ; mais pour juger des remords d'autrui, ce sentiment qui est dans nous est insuffisant : c'est pourquoi il en faut croire les autres hommes sur leur parole, ou sur les signes sensibles et extérieurs que nous avons remarqués en nous-mêmes, lorsque nous éprouvions la même conscience et les mêmes tourments.

Mais pour décider si les animaux qui ne parlent point ont reçu la loi naturelle, il faut s'en rapporter

conséquemment à ces signes dont je viens de **parler,**
supposé qu'ils existent. Les faits semblent le prouver. Le chien qui a mordu son maître qui l'agaçait,
a paru s'en repentir le moment suivant; on l'a vu
triste, fâché, n'osant se montrer, et s'avouer coupable
par un air rampant et humilié. L'histoire nous
offre un exemple célèbre d'un lion qui ne voulut
pas déchirer un homme abandonné à sa fureur,
parce qu'il le reconnut pour son bienfaiteur. Qu'il
serait à souhaiter que l'homme même montrât toujours la même reconnaissance pour les bienfaits et
le même respect pour l'humanité ! On n'aurait plus
à craindre les ingrats, ni ces guerres qui sont le fléau
du genre humain et les vrais bourreaux de la loi
naturelle.

Mais un être à qui la nature a donné un instinct
si précoce, si éclairé, qui juge, combine, raisonne et
délibère, autant que s'étend et le lui permet la sphère
de son activité; un être qui s'attache par les bienfaits, qui se détache par les mauvais traitements et
va essayer un meilleur maître; un être d'une structure semblable à la nôtre, qui fait les mêmes opérations, qui a les mêmes passions, les mêmes douleurs, les mêmes plaisirs, plus ou moins vifs suivant l'empire de l'imagination et la délicatesse des
nerfs; un tel être enfin ne montre-t-il pas clairement
qu'il sent ses torts et les nôtres, qu'il connait le
bien et le mal et, en un mot, a conscience de ce qu'il
fait? Son âme qui marque comme la nôtre les
mêmes joies, les mêmes mortifications, les mêmes
déconcertements, serait-elle sans aucune répugnance
à la vue de son semblable déchiré, ou après l'avoir
lui-même impitoyablement mis en pièces? Cela posé,
le don précieux dont il s'agit n'aurait point été

refusé aux animaux ; car puisqu'ils nous offrent des signes évidents de leur repentir, comme de leur intelligence, qu'y a-t-il d'absurde à penser que des êtres, des machines presque aussi parfaites que nous, soient, comme nous, faites pour penser et pour sentir la nature ?

Qu'on ne m'objecte point que les animaux sont pour la plûpart des êtres féroces, qui ne sont pas capables de sentir les maux qu'ils font ; car tous les hommes distinguent-ils mieux les vices et les vertus ? Il est dans notre espèce de la férocité, comme dans la leur. Les hommes qui sont dans la barbare habitude d'enfreindre la loi naturelle, n'en sont pas si tourmentés que ceux qui la transgressent pour la première fois, et que la force de l'exemple n'a point endurcis. Il en est de même des animaux, comme des hommes. Les uns et les autres peuvent être plus ou moins féroces par tempérament, et ils le deviennent encore plus avec ceux qui le sont. Mais un animal doux, pacifique, qui vit avec d'autres animaux semblables, et d'aliments doux, sera ennemi du sang et du carnage, il rougira intérieurement de l'avoir versé ; avec cette différence peut-être que, comme chez eux tout est immolé aux besoins, aux plaisirs et aux commodités de la vie, dont ils jouissent plus que nous, leurs remords ne semblent pas devoir être si vifs que les nôtres, parceque nous ne sommes pas dans la même nécessité qu'eux. La coutume émousse et peut-être étouffe les remords, comme les plaisirs.

Mais je veux pour un moment supposer que je me trompe, et qu'il n'est pas juste que presque tout l'univers ait tort à ce sujet, tandis que j'aurais seul raison ; j'accorde que les animaux, même les plus

excellents, ne connaissent pas la distinction du bien
et du mal moral, qu'ils n'ont aucune mémoire des
attentions qu'on a eues pour eux, du bien qu'on leur
a fait, aucun sentiment de leurs propres vertus;
que ce lion, par exemple, dont j'ai parlé après tant
d'autres, ne se souvienne pas de n'avoir pas voulu
ravir la vie à cet homme qui fut livré à sa furie,
dans un spectacle plus inhumain que tous les lions,
les tigres et les ours; tandis que nos compatriotes
se battent, Suisses contre Suisses, frères contre
frères, se reconnaissent, s'enchaînent, ou se tuent
sans remords, parce qu'un prince paie leurs meur-
tres: je suppose enfin que la loi naturelle n'ait pas
été donnée aux animaux, quelles en seront les conséquences? L'homme n'est pas pétri d'un limon
plus précieux; la nature n'a employé qu'une seule
et même pâte, dont elle a seulement varié les levains.
Si donc l'animal ne se repent pas d'avoir violé le
sentiment intérieur dont je parle, ou plutôt s'il en
est absolument privé, il faut nécessairement que
l'homme soit dans le même cas: moyennant quoi
adieu la loi naturelle et tous ces beaux traités
qu'on a publiés sur elle! Tout le règne animal en
serait généralement dépourvû. Mais réciproquement
si l'homme ne peut se dispenser de convenir qu'il
distingue toujours, lorsque la santé le laisse jouïr
de lui-même, ceux qui ont de la probité, de l'humanité, de la vertu, de ceux qui ne sont ni humains, ni
vertueux, ni honnêtes gens; qu'il est facile de distinguer ce qui est vice, ou vertu, par l'unique plaisir
ou la propre répugnance qui en sont comme les
effets naturels, il s'ensuit que les animaux formés
de la même matière, à laquelle il n'a peut-être manqué qu'un degré de fermentation pour égaler les

hommes en tout, doivent participer aux mêmes
prérogatives de l'animalité, et qu'ainsi il n'est point
d'âme, ou de substance sensitive, sans remords. La
réflexion suivante va fortifier celles-ci.

On ne peut détruire la loi naturelle. L'empreinte en est si forte dans tous les animaux, que
je ne doute nullement que les plus sauvages et les
plus féroces n'aient quelques moments de repentir.
Je crois que la fille sauvage de Châlons en Champagne aura porté la peine de son crime, s'il est vrai
qu'elle ait mangé sa sœur. Je pense la même chose
de tous ceux qui commettent des crimes, même
involontaires, ou de tempérament : de Gaston d'Or-
léans qui ne pouvait s'empêcher de voler ; de certaine femme qui fut sujette au même vice dans la
grossesse, et dont ses enfants héritèrent ; de celle qui
dans le même état, mangea son mari ; de cette autre
qui égorgeait les enfants, salait leurs corps, et en
mangeait tous les jours comme du petit salé ; de
cette fille de voleur anthropophage, qui la devint
à 12 ans, quoiqu'ayant perdu père et mère à l'âge
d'un an elle eût été élevée par d'honnêtes gens,
pour ne rien dire de tant d'autres exemples dont nos
observateurs sont remplis, et qui prouvent tous
qu'il est mille vices et vertus héréditaires, qui
passent des parents aux enfants, comme ceux de la
nourrice à ceux qu'elle allaite. Je dis donc et j'accorde que ces malheureux ne sentent pas pour la
plupart sur le champ l'énormité de leur action. La
boulimie, par exemple, ou la faim canine, peut éteindre tout sentiment ; c'est une manie d'estomac qu'on
est forcé de satisfaire. Mais revenues à elles-mêmes,
et comme désenivrées, quels remords pour ces
femmes qui se rappellent le meurtre qu'elles ont

commis dans ce qu'elles avaient de plus cher! quelle punition d'un mal involontaire, auquel elles n'ont pu résister, dont elles n'ont eu aucune conscience! Cependant ce n'est point assez apparemment pour les juges. Parmi les femmes dont je parle, l'une fut rouée, et brûlée, l'autre enterrée vive. Je sens tout ce que demande l'intérêt de la société. Mais il serait sans doute à souhaiter qu'il n'y eût pour juges que d'excellents médecins. Eux seuls pourraient distinguer le criminel innocent, du coupable. Si la raison est esclave d'un sens dépravé, ou en fureur, comment peut-elle le gouverner?

Mais si le crime porte avec soi sa propre punition plus ou moins cruelle; si la plus longue et la plus barbare habitude ne peut tout-à-fait arracher le repentir des cœurs les plus inhumains; s'ils sont déchirés par la mémoire même de leurs actions; pour quoi effrayer l'imagination des esprits faibles par un enfer, par des spectres, et des précipices de feu, moins réels encore que ceux de Pascal*? Qu'est-il besoin de recourir à des fables, comme un pape de bonne foi l'a dit lui-mème, pour tourmenter les malheureux mêmes qu'on fait périr, parce qu'on ne les trouve pas assez punis par leur propre conscience, qui est leur premier bourreau? Ce n'est pas que je veuille dire que tous les criminels soient injuste-

---

*Dans un cercle, ou à table, il lui fallait toujours un rempart de chaises, ou quelqu'un dans son voisinage du côté gauche, pour l'empêcher de voir des abimes épouvantables dans lesquels il craignait quelquefois de tomber, quelque connaissance qu'il eut de ces illusions. Quel effrayant effet de l'imagination, ou d'une singulière circulation dans un lobe du cerveau! Grand homme d'un côté, il était à moitié fou de l'autre. La folie et la sagesse avaient chacun leur département, ou leur *lobe,* séparé par la *faux.* De quel côté tenait-il si fort à Mrs. de Port-Royal? J'ai lu ce fait dans un extrait du *traité du vertige* de Mr. de la Mettrie.

ment punis ; je prétends seulement que ceux dont la
volonté est dépravée, et la conscience éteinte, le
sont assez par leurs remords, quand ils reviennent
à eux-mêmes ; remords, j'ose encore le dire, dont
la nature aurait dû en ce cas, ce me semble, dé-
livrer des malheureux entraînés par une fatale nécessité.

Les criminels, les méchants, les ingrats, ceux
enfin que ne sentent pas la nature, tyrans malheureux et indignes du jour, ont beau se faire un
cruel plaisir de leur barbarie, il est des moments
calmes et de réflexion, où la conscience vengeresse
s'élève, dépose contr'eux, et les condamne à être
presque sans cesse déchirés de ses propres mains.
Qui tourmente les hommes, est tourmenté par lui-
même ; et les maux qu'il sentira seront la juste mesure de ceux qu'il aura faits.

D'un autre côté, il y a tant de plaisir à faire du
bien, à sentir, à reconnaître celui qu'on reçoit, tant
de contentement à pratiquer la vertu, à être doux,
humain, tendre, charitable, compatissant et généreux (ce seul mot renferme toutes les vertus), que
je tiens pour assez puni quiconque a le malheur de
n'être pas né vertueux.

Nous n'avons pas originairement été faits pour être
savants ; c'est peut-être par une espèce d'abus de nos
facultés organiques, que nous le sommes devenus ;
et cela à la charge de l'Etat, qui nourrit une multitude de fainéants, que la vanité a decorés du nom
de *philosophes*. La nature nous a tous créés uni-
quement pour être heureux ; oui, tous, depuis le ver
qui rampe, jusqu'à l'aigle qui se perd dans la nue.
C'est pourquoi elle a donné à tous les animaux
quelque portion de la loi naturelle, portion plus

ou moins exquise selon que le comportent les organes bien conditionnés de chaque animal.

A présent, comment définirons-nous la loi naturelle? C'est un sentiment qui nous apprend ce que nous ne devons pas faire, parce que nous ne voudrions pas qu'on nous le fît. Oserais-je ajouter à cette idée commune, qu'il me semble que ce sentiment n'est qu'une espèce de crainte, ou de frayeur, aussi salutaire à l'espèce qu'a l'individu; car peut-être ne respectons-nous la bourse et la vie des autres, que pour nous conserver nos biens, notre honneur et nous-mêmes; semblables à ces *Ixions du Christianisme* qui n'aiment Dieu et n'embrassent tant de chimériques vertus, que parce qu'ils craignent l'enfer.

Vous voyez que la loi naturelle n'est qu'un sentiment intime, qui appartient encore à l'imagination, comme tous les autres, parmi lesquels on compte la pensée. Par conséquent elle ne suppose évidemment ni éducation, ni révélation, ni législateur, à moins qu'on ne veuille la confondre avec les lois civiles, à la manière ridicule des théologiens.

Les armes du fanatisme peuvent détruire ceux qui soutiennent ces vérités; mais elles ne détruiront jamais ces vérités mêmes.

Ce n'est pas que je révoque en doute l'existence d'un Etre suprême; il me semble au contraire que le plus grand degré de probabilité est pour elle: mais comme cette existence ne prouve pas plus la nécessité d'un culte, que toute autre, c'est une vérité théorique, qui n'est guère d'usage dans la pratique: de sorte que, comme on peut dire, d'après tant d'expériences, que la religion ne suppose pas l'exacte probité, les mêmes raisons autorisent à penser que l'athéisme ne l'exclut pas.

Qui sait d'ailleurs si la raison de l'existence de l'homme ne serait pas dans son existence même? Peut-être a-t-il été jeté au hasard sur un point de la surface de la terre, sans qu'on puisse savoir ni comment, ni pourquoi, mais seulement qu'il doit vivre et mourir, semblable à ces champignons, qui paraissent d'un jour à l'autre, ou à ces fleurs qui bordent les fossés et couvrent les murailles.

Ne nous perdons point dans l'infini, nous ne sommes pas faits pour en avoir la moindre idée; il nous est absolument impossible de remonter à l'origine des choses. Il est égal d'ailleurs pour notre repos, que la matière soit éternelle, ou qu'elle ait été créée, qu'il y ait un Dieu, ou qu'il n'y en ait pas. Quelle folie de tant se tourmenter pour ce qu'il est impossible de connaître, et ce qui ne nous rendrait pas plus heureux, quand nous en viendrions à bout.

Mais, dit-on, lisez tous les ouvrages des Fénelon, des Nieuventit, des Abadie, des Derham, des Raï, etc. Eh bien! que m'apprendront-ils? ou plutôt que m'ont-ils appris? Ce ne sont que d'ennuyeuses répétitions d'écrivains zélés, dont l'un n'ajoute à l'autre qu'un verbiage, plus propres à fortifier qu'à saper les fondements de l'athéisme. Le volume des preuves qu'on tire du spectacle de la nature, ne leur donne pas plus de force. La structure seule d'un doigt, d'une oreille, d'un œil, *une observation de Malpighi,* prouve tout, et sans doute beaucoup mieux que *Descartes* et *Malebranche*; ou tout le reste ne prouve rien. Les déistes, et les Chrétiens mêmes devraient donc se contenter de faire observer

que, dans tout le règne animal, les mêmes vues sont
exécutées par une infinité de divers moyens, tous
cependant exactement géométriques. Car de quelles
plus fortes armes pourrait-on terrasser les athées?
Il est vrai que si ma raison ne me trompe pas,
l'homme et tout l'univers semblent avoir été des-
tinés à cette unité de vues. Le soleil, l'air, l'eau,
l'organisation, la forme des corps, tout est arrangé
dans l'œil, comme dans un miroir qui présente fidèle-
ment à l'imagination les objets qui y sont peints,
suivant les lois qu'exige cette infinie variété de
corps qui servent à la vision. Dans l'oreille, nous
trouvons partout une diversité frappante, sans que
cette diverse fabrique de l'homme, des animaux,
des oiseaux, des poissons, produise différents usages.
Toutes les oreilles sont si mathématiquement faites,
qu'elles tendent également au seul et même but, qui
est d'entendre. Le hasard, demande le déiste,
serait-il donc assez grand géomètre, pour varier
ainsi à son gré les ouvrages dont on le suppose
auteur, sans que tant de diversité pût l'empêcher
d'atteindre la même fin? Il objecte encore ces parties évidemment contenues dans l'animal pour de
futurs usages, le papillon dans la chenille, l'homme
dans le ver spermatique, un polype entier dans
chacune de ses parties, la valvule du trou ovale,
le poumon dans le fœtus, les dents dans leurs alvé-
oles, les os dans les fluides, qui s'en détachent et se
durcissent d'une manière incompréhensible. Et
comme les partisans de ce système, loin de rien
négliger pour le faire valoir, ne se lassent jamais
d'accumuler preuves sur preuves, ils veulent profiter de tout, et de la faiblesse même de l'esprit en
certain cas. Voyez, disent-ils, les Spinoza, les Va-

nini, les Desbarreaux. les Boindin, apôtres qui font plus d'honneur que de tort au déisme! La durée de la santé de ces derniers a été la mesure de leur incrédulité: et il est rare en effet, ajoutent-ils, qu'on n'abjure pas l'athéisme, dès que les passions se sont affaiblies avec le corps qui en est l'instrument.

Voilà certainement tout ce qu'on peut dire de plus favorable à l'existence d'un Dieu, quoique le dernier argument soit frivole, en ce que ces conversions sont courtes, l'esprit reprenant presque toujours ses anciennes opinions et se conduisant en conséquence, dès qu'il a recouvré ou plutôt retrouvé ses forces dans celles du corps. En voilà du moins beaucoup plus que n'en dit le médecin *Diderot* dans ses *Pensées philosophiques,* sublime ouvrage qui ne convaincra pas un athée. Que répondre en effet à un homme qui dit? "Nous ne connaissons point "la nature: des causes cachées dans son sein pour-"raient avoir tout produit. Voyez à votre tour le "polype de Trembley! ne contient-il pas en soi les "causes qui donnent lieu à sa régénération? quelle "absurdité y aurait-il donc à penser qu'il est des "causes physiques pour lesquelles tout a été fait, et "auxquelles toute la chaîne de ce vaste univers est "si nécessairement liée et assujettie, que rien de ce "qui arrive ne pouvait pas ne pas arriver; des causes "dont l'ignorance absolument invincible nous a fait "recourir à un Dieu, qui n'est pas même un *être de* "*raison,* suivant certains? Ainsi, détruire le ha-"sard, ce n'est pas prouver l'existence d'un Etre su-"prême, puisqu'il peut y avoir autre chose qui ne "serait ni hasard, ni Dieu, je veux dire la Nature, "dont l'étude par conséquent ne peut faire que des

"incrédules, comme le prouve la façon de penser de
"tous ses plus heureux scrutateurs."

Le *poids de l'univers* n'ébranle donc pas un véritable athée, loin de *l'écraser*; et tous ces indices
mille et mille fois rebattus d'un Créateur, indices
qu'on met fort au-dessus de la façon de penser dans
nos semblables, ne sont évidents, quelque loin qu'on
pousse cet argument, que pour les Antipyrrhoniens,
ou pour ceux qui ont assez de confiance dans leur
raison pour croire pouvoir juger sur certaines ap-
parences, auxquelles, comme vous voyez, les athées
peuvent en opposer d'autres peut-être aussi fortes
et absolument contraires. Car si nous écoutons encore les naturalistes, ils nous diront que les mêmes
causes qui dans les mains d'un chimiste et par le
hasard de divers mélanges ont fait le premier miroir, dans celles de la nature ont fait l'eau pure, qui
en sert à la simple bergère: que le mouvement qui
conserve le monde, a pu le créer; que chaque corps
a pris la place que sa nature lui a assignée; que
l'air a dû entourer la terre, par la même raison que
le fer et les autres métaux sont l'ouvrage de ses
entrailles; que le soleil est une production aussi
naturelle, que celle de l'électricité; qu'il n'a pas plus
été fait pour échauffer la terre et tous ses habitants,
qu'il brûle quelquefois, que la pluie pour faire pous-
ser les grains, qu'elle gâte souvent; que le miroir et
l'eau n'ont pas plus été faits pour qu'on pût s'y regarder, que tous les corps polis qui ont la même
propriété: que l'œil est à la vérité une espèce de
trumeau dans lequel l'âme peut contempler l'image
des objets, tels qu'ils lui sont représentés par ces
corps: mais qu'il n'est pas démontré que cet organe
ait été réellement fait exprès pour cette contem-

plation, ni exprès placé dans l'orbite ; qu'enfin il se
pourrait bien faire que Lucrèce, le médecin Lamy
et tous les Epicuriens anciens et modernes eûssent
raison, lorsqu'ils avancent que l'œil ne voit que par
ce qu'il se trouve organisé, et placé comme il l'est,
que posées une fois les mêmes règles de mouvement
que suit la nature dans la génération et le développement des corps, il n'était pas possible que ce merveilleux organe fût organisé et placé autrement.

Tel est le pour et le contre, et l'abrégé des grandes
raisons qui partageront éternellement les philosophes. Je ne prends aucun parti.

"Non nostrum inter vos tantas componere lites."

C'est ce que je disais à un Français de mes amis,
aussi franc Pyrrhonien que moi, homme de beaucoup de mérite, et digne d'un meilleur sort. Il me
fit à ce sujet une réponse fort singulière. Il est
vrai, me dit-il, que le pour et le contre ne doit
point inquiéter l'âme d'un philosophe, qui voit que
rien n'est démontré avec assez de clarté pour forcer
son consentement, et même que les idées indicatives
qui s'offrent d'un côté, sont ausitôt détruites par
celles qui se montrent de l'autre. Cependant, re-
prit-il, l'univers ne sera jamais heureux, à moins
qu'il ne soit athée. Voici quelles étaient les raisons
de cet *abominable* homme. Si l'athéisme, disait-
il, était généralement répandu, toutes les branches
de la religion seraient alors détruites et coupées
par la racine. Plus de guerres théologiques ; plus
de soldats de religion ; soldats terribles ! la nature
infectée d'un poison sacré, reprendrait ses droits et
sa pureté. Sourds à toute autre voix, les mortels
tranquilles ne suivraient que les conseils spontanés

de leur propre individu, les seuls qu'on ne méprise point impunément et qui peuvent seuls nous conduire au bonheur par les agréables sentiers de la vertu.

Telle est la loi naturelle; quiconque en est rigide observateur, est honnête homme, et mérite la confiance de tout le genre humain. Quiconque ne la suit pas scrupuleusement, a beau affecter les spécieux dehors d'une autre religion, est un fourbe, ou un hypocrite dont je me défie.

Après cela, qu'un vain peuple pense différemment; qu'il ose affirmer qu'il y va de la probité même, à ne pas croire la Révélation; qu'il faut en un mot un autre religion que celle de la nature, quelle qu'elle soit! quelle misère! quelle pitié! et la bonne opinion que chacun nous donne de celle qu'il a embrassée! Nous ne briguons point ici le suffrage du vulgaire. Qui dresse dans son cœur des autels à la superstition, est né pour adorer des idoles, et non pour sentir la vertu.

Mais puisque toutes les facultés de l'âme dépendent tellement de la propre organisation du cerveau et de tout le corps, qu'elles ne sont visiblement que cette organisation même: voilà une machine bien éclairée! car enfin quand l'homme seul aurait reçu en partage la loi naturelle, en serait-il moins une machine? Des roues, quelques ressorts de plus que dans les animaux les plus parfaits, le cerveau proportionnellement plus proche du cœur, et recevant aussi plus de sang, la même raison donnée; que sais-je enfin? des causes inconnues produiraient toujours cette conscience délicate, si facile à blesser, ces remords qui ne sont pas plus étrangers à la matière que la pensée, et en un mot toute la différence qu'on suppose ici. L'organisation suffirait-elle donc a tout? oui, encore une fois. Puisque la pensée se développe visiblement avec les organes, pourquoi la matière dont ils sont faits ne serait-elle pas aussi susceptible de remords, quand une fois elle a acquis avec le temps la faculté de sentir?

L'âme n'est donc qu'un vain terme dont on n'a point d'idée, et dont un bon esprit ne doit se servir que pour nommer la partie qui pense en nous. Posé le moindre principe de mouvement, les corps animés auront tout ce qu'il leur faut pour se mouvoir, sentir, penser, se repentir, et se conduire en un mot dans le physique, et dans le moral qui en dépend.

Nous ne supposons rien; ceux qui croiraient que toutes les difficultés ne seraient pas encore levées, vont trouver des expériences, qui achèveront de les satisfaire.

1. Toutes les chairs des animaux palpitent après la mort, d'autant plus longtemps que l'animal est plus froid et transpire moins : les tortues, les lézards, les serpents, etc. en font foi.

2. Les muscles séparés du corps, se retirent, lorsqu'on les pique.

3. Les entrailles conservent longtemps leur mouvement péristaltique, ou vermiculaire.

4. Une simple injection d'eau chaude ranime le cœur et les muscles, suivant Cowper.

5. Le cœur de la grenouille, surtout exposé au soleil, encore mieux sur une table ou une assiette chaude, se remue pendant une heure et plus, après avoir été arraché du corps. Le mouvement semble-t-il perdu sans ressource? il n'y a qu'à piquer le cœur, et ce muscle creux bat encore. Harvey a fait la même observation sur les crapauds.

6. Bacon de Verulam, dans son Traité *Sylva-*

Sylvarum, parle d'un homme convaincu de trahison, qu'on ouvrit vivant, et dont le cœur jeté dans l'eau chaude sauta à plusieurs reprises, toujours moins haut, à la distance perpendiculaire de 2 pieds.

7. Prenez un petit poulet encore dans l'œuf; arrachez lui le cœur; vous observerez les mêmes phénomènes, avec à peu près les mêmes circonstances. La seule chaleur de l'haleine ranime un animal prêt à périr dans la machine pneumatique.

Les mêmes expériences que nous devons à Boyle et à Sténon, se font dans les pigeons, dans les chiens, dans les lapins, dont les morceaux de cœur se remuent, comme les cœurs entiers. On voit le même mouvement dans les pattes de taupe arrachées.

8. La chenille, les vers, l'araignée, la mouche, l'anguille offrent les mêmes choses à considérei; et le mouvement des parties coupées augmente dans l'eau chaude, à cause du feu qu'elle contient.

9. Un soldat ivre emporta d'un coup de sabre la tête d'un coq d'Inde. Cet animal resta debout, ensuite il marcha, courut; venant à rencontrer une muraille, il se tourna, battit des ailes, en continuant de courir, et tomba enfin. Etendu par terre, tous les muscles de ce coq se remuaient encore. Voilà ce que j'ai vu, et il est facile de voir à peu près ces phénomènes dans les petits chats, ou chiens, dont on a coupé la tête.

10. Les polypes font plus que de se mouvoir, après la section; ils se reproduisent dans huit jours en autant d'animaux qu'il y a de parties coupées. J'en suis fâché pour le système des naturalistes sur la génération, ou plutôt j'en suis bien aise; car que cette découverte nous apprend bien à ne jamais rien

conclure de général, même de toutes les expériences connues, et les plus décisives!

Voilà beaucoup plus de faits qu'il n'en faut, pour prouver d'une manière incontestable que chaque petite fibre, ou partie des corps organisés, se meut par un principe qui lui est propre, et dont l'action ne dépend point des nerfs, comme les mouvements volontaires, puisque les mouvements en question s'exercent sans que les parties qui les manifestent aient aucun commerce avec la circulation. Or, si cette force se fait remarquer jusques dans des morceaux de fibres, le cœur, qui est un composé de fibres singulièrement entrelacées, doit avoir la même propriété. L'histoire de Bacon n'était pas nécessaire pour me le persuader. Il m'était facile d'en juger, et par la parfaite analogie de la structure du cœur de l'homme et des animaux; et par la masse même du premier, dans laquelle ce mouvement ne se cache aux yeux, que parce qu'il y est étouffé; et enfin parce que tout est froid et affaissé dans les cadavres. Si les dissections se faisaient sur des criminels suppliciés, dont les corps sont encore chauds, on verrait dans leur cœur les mêmes mouvements qu'on observe dans les muscles du visage des gens décapités.

Tel est ce principe moteur des corps entiers, ou des parties coupées en morceaux, qu'il produit des mouvements non déréglés, comme on l'a cru, mais très réguliers, et cela, tant dans les animaux chauds et parfaits, que dans ceux qui sont froids et imparfaits. Il ne reste donc aucune ressource à nos adversaires, si ce n'est que de nier mille et mille faits que chacun peut facilement vérifier.

Si on me demande à présent quel est le siége de

cette force innée dans nos corps, je réponds qu'elle
réside très clairement dans ce que les anciens ont
appellé *parenchyme*; c'est à dire dans la substance
propre des parties, abstraction faite des veines, des
artères, des nerfs, en un mot de l'organisation de
tout le corps; et que par conséquent chaque partie
contient en soi des ressorts plus ou moins vifs, selon
le besoin qu'elles en avaient.

Entrons dans quelque détail de ces ressorts de la
machine humaine. Tous les mouvements vitaux, animaux, naturels et automatiques se font par leur
action.　N'est-ce pas machinalement que le corps
se retire, frappé de terreur à l'aspect d'un précipice
inattendu? que les paupières se baissent à la menace
d'un coup, comme on l'a dit? que la *pupille* s'étrécit
au grand jour pour conserver la rétine, et s'élargit
pour voir les objets dans l'obscurité? n'est-ce pas
machinalement que les pores de la peau se ferment
en hiver, pour que le froid ne pénètre pas l'intérieur des vaisseaux? que l'estomac se soulève, irrité
par le poison, par une certaine quantité d'opium,
par tous les émétiques, etc.? que le cœur, les artères,
les muscles se contractent pendant le sommeil,
comme pendant la veille? que le poumon fait l'of-
fice d'un souflet continuellement exercé? n'est-ce pas
machinalement qu'agissent tous les sphincters de
la vessie, du *rectum*, etc.? que le cœur a une con-
traction plus forte que tout autre muscle? que les
muscles érecteurs font dresser la verge dans
l'homme, comme dans les animaux qui s'en battent
le ventre, et même dans l'enfant, capable d'érection,
pour peu que cette partie soit irritée? Ce qui prouve,
pour le dire en passant, qu'il est un ressort singulier
dans ce membre, encore peu connu, et qui produit

des effets qu'on n'a point encore bien expliqués, malgré toutes les lumières de l'anatomie.

Je ne m'étendrai pas davantage sur tous ces petits
ressorts subalternes connus de tout le monde. Mais
il en est un autre plus subtil, et plus merveilleux
qui les anime tous; il est la source de tous nos
sentiments, de tous nos plaisirs, de toutes nos passions, de toutes nos pensées; car le cerveau a ses
muscles pour penser, comme les jambes pour mar-
cher. Je veux parler de ce principe incitant, et
impétueux, qu'Hippocrate appelle ἐνορμῶν (l'âme).
Ce principe existe, et il a son siège dans le cerveau
à l'origine des nerfs, par lesquels il exerce son empire sur tout le reste du corps. Par là s'explique
tout ce qui peut s'expliquer, jusqu'aux effets sur-
prenants des maladies de l'imagination.

Mais, pour ne pas languir dans une richesse et
une fécondité mal entendue, il faut se borner à un
petit nombre de questions et de réflexions.

Pourquoi la vue ou la simple idée d'une belle
femme nous cause-t-elle des mouvements et des désirs
singuliers? Ce qui se passe alors dans certains organes, vient-il de la nature même de ces organes?
Point du tout; mais du commerce et de l'espèce de
sympathie de ces muscles avec l'imagination, Il n'y
a ici qu'un premier ressort excité par le *bene placi-
tum* des anciens, ou par l'image de la beauté, qui
en excite un autre, lequel était fort assoupi, quand
l'imagination l'a éveillé : et comment cela, si ce n'est
par le désordre et le tumulte du sang et des esprits,
qui galopent avec une promptitude extraordinaire,
et vont gonfler les corps caverneux?

Puisqu'il est des communications évidentes entre

la mère et l'enfant*, et qu'il est dur de nier des
faits rapportés par Tulpius et par d'autres écrivains
aussi dignes de foi (il n'y en a point qui le soient
plus), nous croirons que c'est par la même voie que le
fœtus ressent l'impétuosité de l'imagination mater-
nelle, comme une cire molle reçoit toutes sortes
d'impressions; et que les mêmes traces, ou envies de
la mère, peuvent s'imprimer sur le fœtus, sans que
cela puisse se comprendre, quoiqu'en disent Blondel
et tous ses adhérents. Ainsi nous faisons réparation
d'honneur au P. Malebranche, beaucoup trop raillé
de sa crédulité par les auteurs qui n'ont point observé d'assez près la nature et ont voulu l'assujettir
à leur idées.

Voyez le portrait de ce fameux Pope, au moins
le Voltaire des Anglais. Les efforts, les nerfs de
son génie sont peints sur sa physionomie; elle est
toute en convulsion; ses yeux sortent de l'orbite,
ses sourcils s'élèvent avec les muscles du front.
Pourquoi? C'est que l'origine des nerfs est en travail et que tout le corps doit se ressentir d'une espèce
d'accouchement aussi laborieux. S'il n'y avait une
corde interne qui tirât ainsi celles du dehors, d'où
viendraient tous ces phénomènes? Admettre une
âme, pour les expliquer, c'est être réduit à l'*opéra-
tion du St. Esprit.*

En effet, si ce qui pense en mon cerveau n'est
pas une partie de ce viscère, et conséquemment de
tout le corps, pourquoi, lorsque tranquille dans mon
lit je forme le plan d'un ouvrage, ou que je poursuis
un raisonnement abstrait, pourquoi mon sang
s'échauffe-t-il? pourquoi la fièvre de mon esprit

---

* Au moins par les vaisseaux. Est-il sûr qu'il n'y en a point
par les nerfs?

passe-t-elle dans mes veines? Demandez-le aux
hommes d'imagination, aux grandes poètes, à ceux
qu'un sentiment bien rendu ravit, qu'un goût exquis,
que les charmes de la nature, de la vérité ou de la
vertu transportent! Par leur enthousiasme, par ce
qu'ils vous diront avoir éprouvé, vous jugerez de la
cause par les effets: par cette *harmonie* que Borelli,
qu'un seul anatomiste a mieux connue que tous les
Leibniziens, vous connaîtrez l'unité matérielle de
l'homme. Car enfin si la tension des nerfs qui fait
la douleur, cause la fièvre, par laquelle l'esprit est
troublé et n'a plus de volonté; et que réciproquement
l'esprit trop exercé trouble le corps, et allume ce
feu de consomption qui a enlevé Bayle dans un âge
si peu avancé; si telle titillation me fait vouloir, me
force de désirer ardemment ce dont je ne me sou-
ciais nullement le moment d'auparavant; si à leur
tour certaines traces du cerveau excitent le même
prurit et les mêmes désirs, pourquoi faire double
ce qui n'est évidemment qu'un? C'est en vain qu'on
se récrie sur l'empire de la volonté. Pour un ordre
qu'elle donne, elle subit cent fois le joug. Et quelle
merveille que le corps obéisse dan l'état sain, puisqu'un torrent de sang et d'esprits vient l'y forcer,
la volonté ayant pour ministres une légion invisible
de fluides plus vifs que l'éclair, et toujours prêts a
la servir! Mais comme c'est par les nerfs que son
pouvoir s'exerce, c'est aussi par eux qu'il est arrêté.
La meilleure volonté d'un amant épuisé, les plus
violents desirs lui rendront-ils sa vigueur perdue?
Hélas! non; et elle en sera la première punie, parceque, posées certaines circonstances, il n'est pas dans
sa puissance de ne pas vouloir du plaisir. Ce que
j'ai dit de la paralysie, etc. revient ici.

La jaunisse vous surprend! ne savez vous pas que
la couleur des corps dépend de celle des verres au
travers desquels on les regarde! Ignorez-vous que
telle est la teinte des humeurs, telle est celle des
objets, au moins par rapport à nous, vains jouets
de mille illusions? Mais ôtez cette teinte de l'humeur
aqueuse de l'œil; faites couler la bile par son tamis
naturel: alors l'âme ayant d'autres yeux, ne verra
plus jaune. N'est ce pas encore ainsi qu'en abattant
la cataracte, ou en injectant le canal d'Eustachi,
on rend la vue aux aveugles, et l'ouie aux sourds?
Combien de gens qui n'étaient peut-être que d'habiles charlatans dans des siècles ignorants, ont passé
pour faire de grands miracles! La belle âme et la
puissante volonté, qui ne peut agir qu'autant que les
dispositions du corps le lui permettent, et dont les
goûts changent avec l'âge et la fièvre! Faut-il donc
s'étonner si les philosophes ont toujours eu en vue
la santé du corps pour conserver celle de l'âme,
si Pythagore a aussi soigneusement ordonné la
diète, que Platon a défendu le vin? Le régime qui
convient au corps, est toujours celui par lequel les
médecins sensés prétendent qu'on doit préluder,
lorsqu'il s'agit de former l'esprit, de l'élever à la
connaissance de la vérité et de la vertu; vains sons
dans le désordre des maladies et le tumulte des
sens! Sans les préceptes de l'hygiène, Epictète,
Socrate, Platon, etc. prêchent en vain: toute morale
est infructueuse, pour qui n'a pas la sobriété en
partage: c'est la source de toutes les vertus comme
l'intempérance est celle de tous les vices.

En faut-il davantage (et pourquoi irais-je me
perdre dans l'histoire des passions, qui toutes s'ex-
pliquent par l'ενορμων d'Hippocrate) pour prouver

que l'homme n'est qu'un animal, ou un assemblage
de ressorts, qui tous se montent les uns par les autres,
sans qu'on puisse dire par quel point du cercle humain la nature a commencé ? Si ces ressorts diffèrent
entr'eux, ce n'est donc que par leur siège et par
quelques degrés de force, et jamais par leur nature ;
et par conséquent l'âme n'est qu'un principe de
mouvement, ou une partie matérielle sensible du
cerveau, qu'on peut, sans craindre l'erreur, regarder
comme un ressort principal de toute la machine, qui
a une influence visible sur tous les autres, et même
parait avoir été fait le premier ; en sorte que tous les
autres n'en seraient qu'une émanation, comme on le
verra par quelques observations que je rapporterai
et qui ont été faites sur divers embryons.

Cette oscillation naturelle, ou propre à notre machine, et dont est douée chaque fibre, et, pour ainsi
dire, chaque élément fibreux, semblable à celle d'une
pendule, ne peut toujours s'exercer. Il faut la re-
nouveler, à mesure qu'elle se perd ; lui donner des
forces, quand elle languit ; l'affaiblir, lorsqu'elle est
opprimée par un excès de force et de vigueur. C'est
en cela seul que la vraie médecine consiste.

Le corps n'est qu'une horloge, dont le nouveau
chyle est l'horloger. Le premier soin de la nature,
quand il entre dans le sang, c'est d'y exciter une
sorte de fièvre, que les chimistes, qui ne rêvent que
fourneaux, ont dû prendre pour une fermentation.
Cette fièvre procure une plus grande filtration
d'esprits, qui machinalement vont animer les muscles et le cœur, comme s'ils y étaient envoyés par
ordre de la volonté.

Ce sont donc les causes ou les forces de la vie
qui entretiennent ainsi durant 100 ans le mouve-

ment perpétuel des solides et des fluides, aussi nécessaire aux uns qu'aux autres. Mais qui peut dire
si les solides contribuent à ce jeu, plus que les
fluides, et *vice versa*? Tout ce qu'on sait, c'est que
l'action des premiers serait bientôt anéantie, sans le
secours des seconds. Ce sont les liqueurs qui par
leur choc éveillent et conservent l'élasticité des vaisseaux, de laquelle dépend leur propre circulation.
De là vient qu'après la mort le ressort naturel de
chaque substance est plus ou moins fort encore suivant les restes de la vie, auxquels il survit, pour ex-
pirer le dernier. Tant il est vrai que cette force des
parties animales peut bien se conserver et s'augmenter par celle de la circulation, mais qu'elle n'en
dépend point, puisqu'elle se passe même de l'inté-
grité de chaque membre, ou viscère, comme on l'a
vu.

Je n'ignore pas que cette opinion n'a pas été
goûtée de tous les savants, et que Stahl surtout l'a
fort dédaignée. Ce grand chimiste a voulu nous
persuader que l'âme était la seule cause de tous nos
mouvements. Mais c'est parler en fanatique, et non
en philosophe.

Pour détruire l'hypothèse Stahlienne, il ne faut
pas faire tant d'efforts que je vois qu'on en a faits
avant moi. Il n'y a qu'à jeter les yeux sur un
joueur de violon. Quelle souplesse! Quelle agilité
dans les doigts! Les mouvements sont si prompts,
qu'il ne paraît presque pas y avoir de succession.
Or, je prie, ou plutôt je défie les Stahliens de me
dire, eux qui connaissent si bien tout ce que peut
notre âme, comment il serait possible qu'elle exé-
cutât si vite tant de mouvements, des mouvements
qui se passent si loin d'elle, et en tant d'endroits

divers. C'est supposer un joueur de flûte qui pourrait faire de brillantes cadences sur une infinité de trous qu'il ne connaitrait pas, et auxquels il ne pourrait seulement pas appliquer le doigt.

Mais disons avec Mr. Hecquet qu'il n'est pas permis à tout le monde d'aller à Corinthe. Et pourquoi Stahl n'aurait-il pas été encore plus favorisé de la nature en qualité d'homme, qu'en qualité de chimiste et de praticien? Il fallait (heureux mortel!) qu'il eût reçu une autre âme que le reste des hommes; une âme souveraine, qui non contente d'avoir quelque empire sur les muscles *volontaires,* tenait sans peine les rênes de tous les mouvements du corps, pouvait les suspendre, les calmer, ou les exciter à son gré. Avec une maitresse aussi despotique, dans les mains de laquelle étaient en quelque sorte les battements du cœur et les lois de la circulation, point de fièvre sans doute; point de douleur; point de langueur; ni honteuse impuissance, ni facheux priapisme. L'âme veut, et les ressorts jouent, se dressent, ou se débandent. Comment ceux de la machine de Stahl se sont-ils sitôt détraqués? Qui a chez soi un si grand médecin, devrait être immortel.

Stahl, au reste, n'est pas le seul qui ait rejeté le principe d'oscillation des corps organisés. De plus grands esprits ne l'ont pas employé, lorsqu'ils ont voulu expliquer l'action du cœur, l'érection du *penis,* etc. Il n'y a qu'à lire les Institutions de médecine de Boerhaave, pour voir quels laborieux et séduisants systèmes, faute d'admettre une force aussi frappante dans tous les corps, ce grand homme a été obligé d'enfanter à la sueur de son puissant génie.

Willis et Perrault, esprits d'une plus faible trempe, mais observateurs assidus de la nature, que le fameux professeur de Leyde n'a connue que par autrui et n'a eue, pour ainsi dire, que de la seconde main, paraissent avoir mieux aimé supposer une âme généralement répandue par tout le corps, que le principe dont nous parlons. Mais dans cette hypothèse qui fut celle de Virgile et de tous les Epicuriens, hypothèse que l'histoire du polype semblerait favoriser à la première vue, les mouvements qui survivent au sujet dans lequel ils sont inhérents viennent d'un *reste d'âme,* que conservent encore les parties qui se contractent, sans être désormais irritées par le sang et les esprits. D'où l'on voit que ces écrivains dont les ouvrages solides éclipsent aisément toutes les fables philosophiques, ne se sont trompés que sur le modèle de ceux qui ont donné à la matière la faculté de penser, je veux dire, pour s'être mal exprimés, en termes obscurs, et qui ne signifient rien. En effet, qu'est ce que ce *reste d'âme,* si ce n'est la force motrice des Leibniziens, mal rendue par une telle expression, et que cependant Perrault surtout a véritablement entrevue. Voy. son *Traité de la Mécanique des Animaux.*

A présent qu'il est clairement démontré contre les Cartésiens, les Stahliens, les Malebranchistes, et les théologiens peu dignes d'être ici placés, que la matière se meut par elle-même, non seulement lorsqu'elle est organisée, comme dans un cœur entier. par exemple, mais lors même que cette organisation est détruite, la curiosité de l'homme voudrait savoir comment un corps, par cela même qu'il est originairement doué d'un souffle de vie, se trouve en conséquence orné de la faculté de sentir, et enfin par celle-ci de la pensée. Et pour en venir à bout, ô bon Dieu, quels efforts n'ont pas faits certains philosophes! et quel galimatias j'ai eu la patience de lire à ce sujet!

Tout ce que l'expérience nous apprend, c'est que tant que le mouvement subsiste, si petit qu'il soit dans une ou plusieurs fibres, il n'y a qu'à les piquer, pour réveiller, animer ce mouvement presque éteint, comme on l'a vu dans cette foule d'expériences dont j'ai voulu accabler les systèmes. Il est donc constant que le mouvement et le sentiment s'excitent tour à tour, et dans les corps entiers, et dans les mêmes corps dont la structure est détruite; pour ne rien dire de certaines plantes qui semblent nous offrir les mêmes phénomènes de la réunion du sentiment et du mouvement.

Mais de plus, combien d'excellents philosophes ont démontré que la pensée n'est qu'une faculté de sentir, et que l'âme raisonnable n'est que l'âme sensitive appliquée à contempler les idées, et à raisonner! Ce qui serait prouvé par cela seul que lorsque le sentiment est éteint, la pensée l'est aussi, comme dans l'apoplexie, la léthargie, la catalepsie, etc. Car ceux qui ont avancé que l'âme n'avait pas moins pensé dans les maladies soporeuses, quoiqu'elle ne se souvint pas des idées qu'elle avait eues, ont soutenu une chose ridicule.

Pour ce qui est de ce développement, c'est une folie de perdre le temps à en rechercher le mécanisme. La nature du mouvement nous est aussi inconnue que celle de la matière. Le moyen de découvrir comment il s'y produit, à moins que de ressusciter avec l'auteur de *l'Histoire de l'Ame* l'ancienne et inintelligible doctrine des *formes substantielles*! Je suis donc aussi consolé d'ignorer comment la matiére, d'inerte et simple, devient active et composée d'organes, que de ne pouvoir regarder le soleil sans verre rouge : et je suis d'aussi bonne composition sur les autres merveilles incompréhensibles de la nature, sur la production du sentiment et de la pensée dans un être qui ne paraissait autrefois à nos yeux bornés qu'un peu de boue.

Qu'on m'accorde seulement que la matière organisée est douée d'un principe moteur, qui seul la différencie de celle qui ne l'est pas (eh! peut-on rien refuser à l'observation la plus incontestable?) et que tout dépend dans les animaux de la diversité de cette organisation, comme je l'ai assez prouvé; c'en est assez pour deviner l'énigme des substances et celle de l'homme. On voit qu'il n'y en a qu'une dans l'univers et que l'homme est la plus parfaite. Il est au singe, aux animaux les plus spirituels, ce que le pendule planétaire de Huygens est à une montre de Julien le Roi. S'il a fallu plus d'instruments, plus de rouages, plus de ressorts pour marquer les mouvements des planètes, que pour marquer les heures, ou les répéter; s'il a fallu plus d'art à Vaucanson pour faire son *Fluteur,* que pour son *Canard,* il eût dû en employer encore davantage pour faire un *Parleur*; machine qui ne peut plus être regardée comme impossible, surtout entre les mains d'un nouveau Prométhée. Il était donc de même nécessaire que la nature employât plus d'art et d'appareil pour faire et entretenir une machine, qui pendant un siècle entier pût marquer tous les battements du cœur et de l'esprit; car si on n'en voit pas au pouls les heures, c'est du moins le baromètre de la chaleur et de la vivacité, par laquelle on peut juger de la nature de l'âme. Je ne me trompe point, le corps humain est une horloge, mais immense, et construite avec tant d'artifice et d'habileté, que si la roue qui sert à marquer les secondes vient à s'arrêter, celle des minutes tourne et va toujours son train, comme la roue des quarts continue de se mouvoir; et ainsi des autres, quand les premières, rouillées, ou dérangées par quelque cause que ce soit, ont interrompu leur marche. Car n'est-ce pas ainsi que l'obstruction de quelques vaisseaux ne suffit pas pour détruire, ou suspendre le fort des mouvements, qui est dans le cœur, comme dans la pièce ouvrière de la machine; puisqu'au contraire les fluides dont le volume est diminué, ayant moins de chemin a faire, le parcourent d'autant plus vîte, emportés comme par un nouveau courant, que la force du cœur s'augmente en raison de la résistance qu'il trouve à l'extrémité des vaisseaux? Lorsque le nerf optique seul comprimé ne laisse plus passer l'image des objets, n'est-ce pas ainsi que la privation de la vue n'empêche pas plus l'usage de l'ouïe, que la privation de ce sens, lorsque les fonctions de la *portion molle* sont interdites, ne suppose celle de l'autre? N'est-ce pas ainsi encore que l'un entend, sans pouvoir dire qu'il entend (si ce n'est après l'attaque du mal) et que l'autre qui n'entend rien, mais dont les nerfs linguaux sont libres dans le cerveau, dit machinalement tous les rêves qui lui passent par la tête? Phénomènes qui ne surprennent point les médecins éclairés. Ils savent à quoi s'en tenir sur la nature de l'homme; et pour le dire en passant: de deux médecins, le meilleur, celui qui mérite le plus de confiance, c'est toujours, à mon avis, celui qui est le plus versé dans la physique, ou la mécanique du corps humain, et qui laissant l'âme et toutes les inquiétudes que cette chimère donne aux sots et aux ignorans, n'est occupé sérieusement que du pur naturalisme.

Laissons donc le prétendu Mr. Charp se moquer des philosophes qui ont regardé les animaux, comme des machines. Que je pense différemment! Je crois que Descartes serait un homme respectable à tous égards, si, né dans un siècle qu'il n'eût pas dû éclairer, il eût connu le prix de l'expérience et de l'observation, et le danger de s'en écarter. Mais il n'est pas moins juste que je fasse ici une authentique réparation à ce grand homme, pour tous ces petits philosophes mauvais plaisants, et mauvais singes de Locke, qui, au lieu de rire impudemment au nez de Descartes, feraient mieux de sentir que sans lui le champ de la philosophie, comme celui du bon esprit sans Newton, serait peut être encore en friche.

Il est vrai que ce célèbre philosophe s'est beaucoup trompé, et personne n'en disconvient. Mais enfin il a connu la nature animale; il a le premier parfaitement démontré que les animaux étaient de pures machines. Or, après une découverte de cette importance et qui suppose autant de sagacité, le moyen, sans ingratitude, de ne pas faire grâce à toutes ses erreurs!

Elles sont à mes yeux toutes réparées par ce grand aveu. Car enfin, quoiqu'il chante sur la distinction des deux substances, il est visible que ce n'est qu'un tour d'adresse, une ruse de style, pour faire avaler aux théologiens un poison caché à l'ombre d'une analogie qui frappe tout le monde, et qu'eux seuls ne voient pas. Car c'est elle, c'est cette forte analogie qui force tous les savants et les vrais juges d'avouer que ces êtres fiers et vains, plus distingués par leur orgueil que par le nom d'hommes, quelque envie qu'ils aient de s'élever, ne sont au fond que des animaux et des machines perpendiculairement rampantes. Elles ont toutes ce merveilleux instinct, dont l'éducation fait de l'esprit, et qui a toujours son siège dans le cerveau, et à son défaut, comme lorsqu'il manque ou est ossifié, dans la moëlle allongée, et jamais dans le cervelet; car je l'ai vu considérablement blessé, d'autres* l'ont trouvé squirreux, sans que l'âme cessât de faire ses fonctions.

Etre machine, sentir, penser, savoir distinguer le bien du mal, comme le bleu du jaune, en un mot être né avec de l'intelligence et un instinct sûr de morale, et n'être qu'un animal, sont donc des choses qui ne sont pas plus contradictoires qu'être un singe ou un perroquet et savoir se donner du plaisir. Car, puisque l'occasion se présente de le dire, qui eut jamais deviné à *priori* qu'une goutte de la liqueur qui se lance dans l'accouplement fit ressentir des plaisirs divins, et qu'il en naîtrait une petite créature, qui pourrait un jour, posées certaines lois, jouir des mêmes délices? Je crois la pensée si peu incompatible avec la matière organisée, qu'elle semble en être une propriété, telle que l'électricité, la faculté motrice, l'impénétrabilité, l'étendue, etc.

Voulez vous de nouvelles observations? En voici qui sont sans réplique et qui prouvent toutes que l'homme ressemble parfaitement aux animaux dans son origine, comme dans tout ce que nous avons déjà cru essentiel de comparer.

J'en appelle à la bonne foi de nos observateurs.

*Haller dans les *Transact. Philosoph.*

Qu'ils nous disent s'il n'est pas vrai que l'homme
dans son principe n'est qu'un ver, qui devient
homme, comme la chenille papillon. Les plus
graves* auteurs nous ont appris comment il faut
s'y prendre pour voir cet animalcule. Tous les
curieux l'ont vu, comme Hartsoeker, dans la semence de l'homme, et non dans celle de la femme;
il n'y a que les sots qui s'en soient fait scrupule.
Comme chaque goutte de sperme contient une infinité
de ces petits vers lorsqu'ils sont lancés à l'ovaire,
il n'y a que le plus adroit, ou le plus vigoureux qui
ait la force de s'insinuer et de s'implanter dans l'œuf
que fournit la femme, et qui lui donne sa première
nourriture. Cet œuf, quelquefois surpris dans les
trompes de Fallope, est porté par ces canaux à la
matrice, où il prend racine, comme un grain de blé
dans la terre. Mais quoiqu'il y devienne monstru-
eux par sa croissance de 9 mois, il ne diffère point
des œufs des autres femelles, si ce n'est que sa peau
(l'*amnios*) ne se durcit jamais, et se dilate prodigieusement, comme on en peut juger en comparant
les fœtus trouvés en situation et près d'éclore (ce
que j'ai eu le plaisir d'observer dans une femme
morte un moment avant l'accouchement), avec
d'autres petits embryons très proches de leur origine : car alors c'est toujours l'œuf dans sa coque,
et l'animal dans l'œuf, qui, gêné dans ses mouvements, cherche machinalement à voir le jour ; et pour
y réussir, il commence par rompre avec la tête cette
membrane, d'où il sort, comme le poulet, l'oiseau,
etc., de la leur. J'ajouterai une observation que je
ne trouve nulle part ; c'est que l'*amnios* n'en est pas
plus mince, pour s'être prodigieusement étendu ;

---

* Boerhaave, *Inst. Med.* et tant d'autres.

semblable en cela à la matrice dont la substance même se gonfle de sucs infiltrés, indépendamment de la réplétion et du déploiement de tous ses coudes vasculeux.

Voyons l'homme dans et hors de sa coque; examinons avec un microscope les plus jeunes embryons, de 4, de 6, de 8 ou de 15 jours; après ce temps les yeux suffisent. Que voit-on? la tête seule; un petit œuf rond avec deux points noirs qui marquent les yeux. Avant ce temps, tout étant plus informe, on n'aperçoit qu'une pulpe médullaire, qui est le cerveau, dans lequel se forme d'abord l'origine des nerfs, ou le principe du sentiment, et le cœur qui a déjà par lui-même dans cette pulpe la faculté de battre: c'est le *punctum saliens* de Malpighi, qui doit peut-être déjà une partie de sa vivacité à l'influence des nerfs. Ensuite peu-à-peu on voit la tête allonger le col, qui en se dilatant forme d'abord le *thorax,* où le cœur a déjà descendu, pour s'y fixer; après quoi vient le bas ventre qu'une cloison (le diaphragme) sépare. Ces dilatations donnent l'une, les bras, les mains, les doigts, les ongles, et les poils; l'autre les cuisses, les jambes, les pieds, etc., avec la seule différence de situation qu'on leur connait, qui fait l'appui et le balancier du corps. C'est une végétation frappante. Ici, ce sont des cheveux qui couvrent le sommet de nos têtes; là, ce sont des feuilles et des fleurs. Partout brille le même luxe de la nature; et enfin l'esprit recteur des plantes est placé où nous avons notre âme, cette autre quintessence de l'homme.

Telle est l'uniformité de la nature qu'on commence à sentir, et l'analogie du règne animal et végétal, de l'homme à la plante. Peut-être même

y a-t-il des plantes animal, c'est-à-dire qui en végé-
tant, ou se battent comme les polypes, ou font d'autres fonctions propres aux animaux?

Voilà à peu près tout ce qu'on sait de la génération. Que les parties qui s'attirent, qui sont faites
pour s'unir ensemble et pour occuper telle ou telle
place, se réunissent toutes suivant leur nature; et
qu'ainsi se forment les yeux, le cœur, l'estomac et
enfin tout le corps, comme de grands hommes l'ont
écrit, cela est possible. Mais, comme l'expérience
nous abandonne au milieu des ces subtilités, je ne
supposerai rien, regardant tout ce qui ne frappe
pas mes sens comme un mystère impénétrable. Il
est si rare que les deux semences se rencontrent
dans le congrès, que je serais tenté de croire que
la semence de la femme est inutile à la génération.

Mais comment en expliquer les phénomènes, sans
ce commode rapport de parties, qui rend si bien raison des ressemblances des enfants, tantôt au père,
et tantôt à la mère? D'un autre côté, l'embarras d'une
explication doit-elle contrebalancer un fait? Il me
parait que c'est le mâle qui fait tout, dans une
femme qui dort, comme dans la plus lubrique.
L'arrangement des parties serait donc fait de toute
éternité dans le germe, ou dans le ver même de
l'homme. Mais tout ceci est fort au-dessus de la
portée des plus excellents observateurs. Comme ils
n'y peuvent rien saisir, ils ne peuvent pas plus juger
de la mécanique de la formation et du développement des corps, qu'une taupe du chemin qu'un cerf
peut parcourir.

Nous sommes de vraies taupes dans le champ
de la nature; nous n'y faisons guères que le trajet
de cet animal; et c'est notre orgueil qui donne des

bornes à ce qui n'en a point. Nous sommes dans le cas d'une montre qui dirait: (un fabuliste en ferait un personnage de conséquence dans un ouvrage frivole) "Quoi! c'est ce sot ouvrier qui m'a "faite, moi qui divise le temps! moi qui marque si "exactement le cours du soleil; moi qui répète à "haute voix les heures que j'indique! non, cela ne "se peut pas." Nous dédaignons de même, ingrats que nous sommes, cette mère commune de tous les *règnes,* comme parlent les chimistes. Nous imaginons ou plutôt supposons une cause supérieure à celle à qui nous devons tout, et qui a véritablement tout fait d'une manière inconcevable. Non, la matière n'a rien de vil, qu'aux yeux grossiers qui la méconnaissent dans ses plus brillants ouvrages; et la nature n'est point une ouvrière bornée. Elle produit des millions d'hommes avec plus de facilité et de plaisir, qu'un horloger n'a de peine à faire la montre la plus composée. Sa puissance éclate également et dans la production du plus vil insecte, et dans celle de l'homme le plus superbe; le règne animal ne lui coûte pas plus que le végétal, ni le plus beau génie qu'un épi de blé. Jugeons donc par ce que nous voyons, de ce qui se dérobe à la curiosité de nos yeux et de nos recherches, et n'imaginons rien au delà. Suivons le singe, le castor, l'éléphant, etc., dans leurs opérations. S'il est évident qu'elles ne peuvent se faire sans intelligence, pourquoi la refuser à ces animaux? et si vous leur accordez une âme, fanatiques, vous êtes perdus; vous aurez beau dire que vous ne décidez point sur sa nature, tandis que vous lui ôtez l'immortalité; qui ne voit que c'est une assertion gratuite? qui ne voit qu'elle doit être ou mortelle, ou immortelle,

comme la nôtre, dont elle doit subir le même sort
quel qu'il soit! et qu'ainsi c'est *tomber dans Scilla
pour vouloir éviter Caribde?*

Brisez la chaîne de vos préjugés; armez-vous du
flambeau de l'expérience et vous ferez à la nature
l'honneur qu'elle mérite, au lieu de rien conclure
à son désavantage, de l'ignorance où elle vous a
laissé. Ouvrez les yeux seulement, et laissez-là ce
que vous ne pouvez comprendre; et vous verrez que
ce laboureur dont l'esprit et les lumières ne
s'étendent pas plus loin que les bords de son sillon,
ne diffère point essentiellement du plus grand génie,
comme l'eût prouvé la dissection des cerveaux de
Descartes et de Newton: vous serez persuadé que
l'imbécile ou le stupide sont des bêtes à figure
humaine, comme le singe plein d'esprit est un
petit homme sous une autre forme; et qu'enfin tout
dépendant absolument de la diversité de l'organisation, un animal bien construit, à qui on a appris
l'astronomie, peut prédire une éclipse, comme la
guérison ou la mort, lorsqu'il a porté quelque temps
du génie et de bons yeux à l'école d'Hippocrate et
au lit des malades. C'est par cette file d'observations et de vérités qu'on parvient à lier à la matière
l'admirable propriété de penser, sans qu'on en puisse
voir les liens, parce que le sujet de cet attribut nous
est essentiellement inconnu.

Ne disons point que toute machine, ou tout animal, périt tout-à-fait, ou prend une autre forme,
après la mort; car nous n'en savons absolument
rien. Mais assurer qu'une machine immortelle est
une chimère, ou un *être de raison,* c'est faire un
raisonnement aussi absurde que celui que feraient
des chenilles, qui, voyant les dépouilles de leurs sem-

blables, déploreraient amèrement le sort de leur
espèce qui leur semblerait s'anéantir. L'âme de
ces insectes (car chaque animal a la sienne) est
trop bornée pour comprendre les métamorphoses
de la nature. Jamais un seul des plus rusés d'entr-
eux n'eût imaginé qu'il dût devenir papillon. Il
en est de même de nous. Que savons-nous plus de
notre destinée, que de notre origine? Soumettons-
nous donc à une ignorance invincible de laquelle
notre bonheur dépend.

Qui pensera ainsi, sera sage, juste, tranquille sur
son sort, et par conséquent heureux. Il attendra
la mort, sans la craindre, ni la désirer; et chérissant
la vie, comprenant à peine comment le dégoût vient
corrompre un cœur dans ce lieu plein de délices;
plein de respect pour la nature, plein de reconnaissance, d'attachement et de tendresse, à proportion du sentiment et des bienfaits qu'il en a reçus,
heureux enfin de la sentir, et d'être au charmant
spectacle de l'univers, il ne le détruira certainement jamais dans soi, ni dans les autres. Que dis-
je! plein d'humanité, il en aimera le caractère jusques dans ses ennemis. Jugez comme il traitera les
autres! Il plaindra les vicieux, sans les haïr; ce
ne seront à ses yeux que des hommes contrefaits.
Mais en faisant grâce aux défauts de la conformation de l'esprit et du corps, il n'en admirera pas
moins leurs beautés et leurs vertus. Ceux que la
nature aura favorisés lui paraîtront mériter plus
d'égards que ceux qu'elle aura traités en marâtre.
C'est ainsi qu'on a vu que les dons naturels, la
source de tout ce qui s'acquiert, trouvent dans la
bouche et le cœur du matérialiste des hommages
que tout autre leur refuse injustement. Enfin le

matérialiste convaincu, quoi que murmure sa propre
vanité, qu'il n'est qu'une machine, ou un animal,
ne maltraitera point ses semblables; trop instruit
sur la nature de ces actions, dont l'inhumanité est
toujours proportionnée au degré d'analogie prouvée
ci devant; et ne voulant pas en un mot, suivant la
loi naturelle donnée à tous les animaux, faire à
autrui ce qu'il ne voudrait pas qu'il lui fît.

Concluons donc hardiment que l'homme est une
machine; et qu'il n'y a dans tout l'univers qu'une
seule substance diversement modifiée. Ce n'est point
ici une hypothèse élevée à force de demandes et de
suppositions: ce n'est point l'ouvrage du préjugé,
ni même de ma raison seule; j'eusse dédaigné un
guide que je crois si peu sûr, si mes sens portant,
pour ainsi dire, le flambeau, ne m'eûssent engagé à
la suivre, en l'éclairant. L'expérience m'a donc
parlé pour la raison; c'est ainsi que je les ai jointes
ensemble.

Mais on a dû voir que je ne me suis permis le
raisonnement le plus rigoureux et le plus immédiate-
ment tiré, qu'à la suite d'une multitude d'observations physiques qu'aucun savant ne contestera; et
c'est encore eux seuls que je reconnais pour juges
des conséquences que j'en tire; récusant ici tout
homme à préjugés, et qui n'est ni anatomiste, ni
au fait de la seule philosophie qui soit ici de mise,
celle du corps humain. Que pourraient contre un
chêne aussi ferme et solide ces faibles roseaux de
la théologie, de la métaphysique et des écoles;
armes puériles, semblables aux fleurets de nos
salles, qui peuvent bien donner le plaisir de l'es-
crime, mais jamais entamer son adversaire. Faut-
il dire que je parle de ces idées creuses et triviales, de

ces raisonnements rebattus et pitoyables, qu'on fera sur la prétendue incompatibilité de deux substances qui se touchent et se remuent sans cesse l'une et l'autre, tant qu'il restera l'ombre du préjugé ou de la superstition sur la terre? Voilà mon système, ou plutôt la vérité, si je ne me trompe fort. Elle est courte et simple. Dispute à présent qui voudra!

MAN A MACHINE.

MAN A MACHINE.

IT is not enough for a wise man to study nature and truth; he should dare state truth for the benefit of the few who are willing and able to think. As for the rest, who are voluntarily slaves of prejudice, they can no more attain truth, than frogs can fly.

I reduce to two the systems of philosophy which deal with man's soul. The first and older system is materialism; the second is spiritualism.

The metaphysicians who have hinted that matter may well be endowed with the faculty of thought[1] have perhaps not reasoned ill. For there is in this case a certain advantage in their inadequate way of expressing their meaning. In truth, to ask whether matter can think, without considering it otherwise than in itself, is like asking whether matter can tell time. It may be foreseen that we shall avoid this reef upon which Locke had the bad luck to shipwreck.

The Leibnizians with their monads have set up an unintelligible hypothesis. They have rather spiritualized matter than materialized the soul. How can we define a being whose nature is absolutely unknown to us?[2]

Descartes and all the Cartesians, among whom the followers of Malebranche have long been numbered, have made the same mistake. They have taken for granted two distinct substances in man, as if they had seen them, and positively counted them.

The wisest men have declared that the soul can not know itself save by the light of faith. However, as reasonable beings they have thought that they could reserve for themselves the right of examining what the Bible means by the word "spirit," which it uses in speaking of the human soul. And if in their investigation, they do not agree with the theologians on this point, are the theologians more in agreement among themselves on all other points?

Here is the result in a few words, of all their reflections. If there is a God, He is the Author of nature as well as of revelation. He has given us the one to explain the other, and reason to make them agree.

To distrust the knowledge that can be drawn from the study of animated bodies, is to regard nature and revelation as two contraries which destroy each the other, and consequently to dare uphold the absurd doctrine, that God contradicts Himself in His various works and deceives us.

If there is a revelation, it can not then contradict nature. By nature only can we understand the meaning of the words of the Gospel, of which experience is the only true interpreter. In fact, the commentators before our time have only obscured the truth. We can judge of this by the author of the "Spectacle of Nature."[3] "It is astonishing," he says concerning Locke, "that a man who degrades our soul far enough to consider it a soul of clay should dare set up reason as judge and sov-

ereign arbiter of the mysteries of faith, for," he
adds, "what an astonishing idea of Christianity
one would have, if one were to follow reason."

Not only do these reflections fail to elucidate
faith, but they also constitute such frivolous objections to the method of those who undertake to
interpret the Scripture, that I am almost ashamed to
waste time in refuting them.

The excellence of reason does not depend on a
big word devoid of meaning (immateriality), but
on the force, extent, and perspicuity of reason itself. Thus a "soul of clay" which should discover,
at one glance, as it were, the relations and the consequences of an infinite number of ideas hard to
understand, would evidently be preferable to a foolish and stupid soul, though that were composed of
the most precious elements. A man is not a philosopher because, with Pliny, he blushes over the
wretchedness of our origin. What seems vile is
here the most precious of things, and seems to be
the object of nature's highest art and most elaborate
care. But as man, even though he should come from
an apparently still more lowly source, would yet be
the most perfect of all beings, so whatever the
origin of his soul, if it is pure, noble, and lofty,
it is a beautiful soul which dignifies the man endowed with it.

Pluche's second way of reasoning seems vicious
to me, even in his system, which smacks a little of
fanaticism; for [on his view] if we have an idea
of faith as being contrary to the clearest principles,
to the most incontestable truths, we must yet conclude, out of respect for revelation and its author,

that this conception is false, and that we do not yet understand the meaning of the words of the Gospel.

Of the two alternatives, only one is possible: either everything is illusion, nature as well as revelation, or experience alone can explain faith. But what can be more ridiculous than the position of our author! Can one imagine hearing a Peripatetic say, "We ought not to accept the experiments of Torricelli,[4] for if we should accept them, if we should rid ourselves of the horror of the void, what an astonishing philosophy we should have!"

I have shown how vicious the reasoning of Pluche is* in order to prove, in the first place, that if there is a revelation, it is not sufficiently demonstrated by the mere authority of the Church, and without any appeal to reason, as all those who fear reason claim: and in the second place, to protect against all assault the method of those who would wish to follow the path that I open to them, of interpreting supernatural things, incomprehensible in themselves, in the light of those ideas with which nature has endowed us. Experience and observation should therefore be our only guides here. Both are to be found throughout the records of the physicians who were philosophers, and not in the works of the philosophers who were not physicians. The former have traveled through and illuminated the labyrinth of man; they alone have laid bare to us those springs [of life] hidden under the external integument which conceals so many wonders from our eyes. They alone, tranquilly contemplating our soul, have surprised it, a thousand times, both in its wretchedness and in its glory, and they have no more despised

*He evidently errs by begging the question.

it in the first estate, than they have admired it in the
second.   Thus, to repeat, only the physicians have
a right to speak on this subject.[5]   What could the
others, especially the theologians, have to say?   Is
it not ridiculous to hear them shamelessly coming
to conclusions about a subject concerning which they
have had no means of knowing anything, and from
which on the contrary they have been completely
turned aside by obscure studies that have led them
to a thousand prejudiced opinions,—in a word, to
fanaticism, which adds yet more to their ignorance
of the mechanism of the body?

But even though we have chosen the best guides,
we shall still find many thorns and stumbling blocks
in the way.

Man is so complicated a machine[6] that it is impossible to get a clear idea of the machine before-
hand, and hence impossible to define it.   For this
reason, all the investigations have been vain, which
the greatest philosophers have made *à priori,* that is
to say, in so far as they use, as it were, the wings
of the spirit.   Thus it is only *à posteriori* or by try-
ing to disentangle the soul from the organs of the
body, so to speak, that one can reach the highest
probability concerning man's own nature, even
though one can not discover with certainty what
his nature is.

Let us then take in our hands the staff of experience,[7] paying no heed to the accounts of all
the idle theories of philosophers.   To be blind and
to think that one can do without this staff is the
worst kind of blindness.   How truly a contemporary
writer says that only vanity fails to gather from
secondary causes the same lessons as from primary

causes! One can and one even ought to admire
all these fine geniuses in their most useless works,
such men as Descartes, Malebranche, Leibniz, Wolff
and the rest, but what profit, I ask, has any one
gained from their profound meditations, and from
all their works? Let us start out then to discover
not what has been thought, but what must be thought
for the sake of repose in life.

There are as many different minds, different characters, and different customs, as there are different
temperaments. Even Galen[8] knew this truth which
Descartes carried so far as to claim that medicine
alone can change minds and morals, along with
bodies. (By the writer of "L'histoire de l'âme,"[9]
this teaching is incorrectly attributed to Hippocrates.[10]) It is true that melancholy, bile, phlegm,
blood etc.—according to the nature, the abundance,
and the different combination of these humors—
make each man different from another.[11]

In disease the soul is sometimes hidden, showing
no sign of life; sometimes it is so inflamed by fury
that it seems to be doubled; sometimes, imbecility
vanishes and the convalescence of an idiot produces a
wise man. Sometimes, again, the greatest genius becomes imbecile and loses the sense of self. Adieu then
to all that fine knowledge, acquired at so high a price,
and with so much trouble! Here is a paralytic who
asks if his leg is in bed with him; there is a soldier
who thinks that he still has the arm which has been
cut off. The memory of his old sensations, and of
the place to which they were referred by his soul,
is the cause of his illusion, and of this kind of de-
lirium. The mere mention of the member which
he has lost is enough to recall it to his mind, and

to make him feel all its motions; and this causes him an indefinable and inexpressible kind of imaginary suffering. This man cries like a child at death's approach, while this other jests. What was needed to change the bravery of Caius Julius, Seneca, or Petronius into cowardice or faintheartedness? Merely an obstruction in the spleen, in the liver, an impediment in the portal vein? Why? Because the imagination is obstructed along with the viscera, and this gives rise to all the singular phenomena of hysteria and hypochondria.

What can I add to the stories already told of those who imagine themselves transformed into wolf-men, cocks or vampires, or of those who think that the dead feed upon them? Why should I stop to speak of the man who imagines that his nose or some other member is of glass? The way to help this man regain his faculties and his own flesh-and-blood nose is to advise him to sleep on hay, lest he break the fragile organ, and then to set fire to the hay that he may be afraid of being burned— a fear which has sometimes cured paralysis. But I must touch lightly on facts which everybody knows.

Neither shall I dwell long on the details of the effects of sleep. Here a tired soldier snores in a trench, in the middle of the thunder of hundreds of cannon. His soul hears nothing; his sleep is as deep as apoplexy. A bomb is on the point of crushing him. He will feel this less perhaps than he feels an insect which is under his foot.

On the other hand, this man who is devoured by jealousy, hatred, avarice, or ambition, can never find any rest. The most peaceful spot, the freshest and most calming drinks are alike useless to one who has not freed his heart from the torment of passion.

The soul and the body fall asleep together. As the motion of the blood is calmed, a sweet feeling of peace and quiet spreads through the whole mechanism. The soul feels itself little by little growing heavy as the eyelids droop, and loses its tenseness, as the fibres of the brain relax; thus little by little it becomes as if paralyzed and with it all the muscles of the body. These can no longer sustain the weight of the head, and the soul can no longer bear the burden of thought; it is in sleep as if it were not.

Is the circulation too quick? the soul can not sleep. Is the soul too much excited? the blood can not be quieted: it gallops through the veins with an audible murmur. Such are the two opposite causes of insomnia. A single fright in the midst of our dreams makes the heart beat at double speed and snatches us from needed and delicious repose, as a real grief or an urgent need would do. Lastly as the mere cessation of the functions of the soul produces sleep, there are, even when we are awake (or at least when we are half awake), kinds of very frequent short naps of the mind, vergers' dreams, which show that the soul does not always wait for the body to sleep. For if the soul is not fast asleep, it surely is not far from sleep, since it can not point out a single object to which it has attended, among the uncounted number of confused ideas which, so to speak, fill the atmosphere of our brains like clouds.

Opium is too closely related to the sleep it produces, to be left out of consideration here. This drug intoxicates, like wine, coffee, etc., each in

its own measure and according to the dose.[12]   It
makes a man happy in a state which would seem-
ingly be the tomb of feeling, as it is the image of
death. How sweet is this lethargy! The soul would
long never to emerge from it. For the soul has been a
prey to the most intense sorrow, but now feels only
the joy of suffering past, and of sweetest peace.
Opium even alters the will, forcing the soul which
wished to wake and to enjoy life, to sleep in spite
of itself. I shall omit any reference to the effect
of poisons.

Coffee, the well-known antidote for wine, by
scourging the imagination, cures our headaches and
scatters our cares without laying up for us, as wine
does, other headaches for the morrow. But let us
contemplate the soul in its other needs.

The human body is a machine which winds its
own springs. It is the living image of perpetual
movement. Nourishment keeps up the movements
which fever excites. Without food, the soul pines
away, goes mad, and dies exhausted. The soul is
a taper whose light flares up the moment before
it goes out. But nourish the body, pour into its
veins life-giving juices and strong liquors, and then
the soul grows strong like them, as if arming itself
with a proud courage, and the soldier whom water
would have made flee, grows bold and runs joy-
ously to death to the sound of drums. Thus a hot
drink sets into stormy movement the blood which
a cold drink would have calmed.

What power there is in a meal! Joy revives in
a sad heart, and infects the souls of comrades, who
express their delight in the friendly songs in which
the Frenchman excels. The melancholy man alone

is dejected, and the studious man is equally out of place [in such company].

Raw meat makes animals fierce, and it would have the same effect on man. This is so true that the English who eat meat red and bloody, and not as well done as ours, seem to share more or less in the savagery due to this kind of food, and to other causes which can be rendered ineffective by education only. This savagery creates in the soul, pride, hatred, scorn of other nations, indocility and other sentiments which degrade the character, just as heavy food makes a dull and heavy mind whose usual traits are laziness and indolence.

Pope understood well the full power of greediness when he said:[13]

> "Catius is ever moral, ever grave,
> Thinks who endures a knave is next a knave,
> Save just at dinner—then prefers no doubt,
> A rogue with ven'son to a saint without."

Elsewhere he says:

> "See the same man in vigor, in the gout
> Alone, in company, in place or out,
> Early at business and at hazard late,
> Mad at a fox chase, wise at a debate,
> Drunk at a borough, civil at a ball,
> Friendly at Hackney, faithless at White Hall."

In Switzerland we had a bailiff by the name of M. Steigner de Wittighofen. When he fasted he was a most upright and even a most indulgent judge, but woe to the unfortunate man whom he found on the culprit's bench after he had had a large dinner! He was capable of sending the innocent like the guilty to the gallows.

We think we are, and in fact we are, good men,

only as we are gay or brave; everything depends
on the way our machine is running. One is sometimes inclined to say that the soul is situated in the
stomach, and that Van Helmont,[14] who said that
the seat of the soul was in the pylorus, made only
the mistake of taking the part for the whole.

To what excesses cruel hunger can bring us! We
no longer regard even our own parents and children. We tear them to pieces eagerly and make
horrible banquets of them; and in the fury with
which we are carried away, the weakest is always
the prey of the strongest.....

One needs only eyes to see the necessary influence
of old age on reason. The soul follows the progress of the body, as it does the progress of education. In the weaker sex, the soul accords also with
delicacy of temperament, and from this delicacy follow tenderness, affection, quick feelings due more
to passion than to reason, prejudices, and superstitions, whose strong impress can hardly be effaced.
Man, on the other hand, whose brain and nerves
partake of the firmness of all solids, has not only
stronger features but also a more vigorous mind.
Education, which women lack, strengthens his mind
still more. Thus with such help of nature and art,
why should not a man be more grateful, more generous, more constant in friendship, stronger in ad-
versity? But, to follow almost exactly the thought
of the author of the "Lettres sur la Physiognomie,"[15] the sex which unites the charms of the
mind and of the body with almost all the tenderest
and most delicate feelings of the heart, should not
envy us the two capacities which seem to have been
given to man, the one merely to enable him better

to fathom the allurements of beauty, and the other
merely to enable him to minister better to its pleasures.

It is no more necessary to be just as great a
physiognomist as this author, in order to guess the
quality of the mind from the countenance or the
shape of the features, provided these are sufficiently
marked, than it is necessary to be a great doctor
to recognize a disease accompanied by all its marked
symptoms. Look at the portraits of Locke, of Steele,
of Boerhaave,[16] of Maupertuis,[17] and the rest, and
you will not be surprised to find strong faces and
eagle eyes. Look over a multitude of others, and you
can always distinguish the man of talent from the
man of genius, and often even an honest man from a
scoundrel. For example, it has been noticed that
a celebrated poet combines (in his portrait) the
look of a pickpocket with the fire of Prometheus.

History provides us with a noteworthy example
of the power of temperature. The famous Duke
of Guise was so strongly convinced that Henry the
Third, in whose power he had so often been, would
never dare assassinate him, that he went to Blois.
When the Chancelor Chiverny learned of the duke's
departure, he cried, "He is lost." After this fatal
prediction had been fulfilled by the event, Chiverny
was asked why he made it. "I have known the
king for twenty years," said he; "he is naturally
kind and even weakly indulgent, but I have noticed
that when it is cold, it takes nothing at all to pro-
voke him and send him into a passion."

One nation is of heavy and stupid wit, and another quick, light and penetrating. Whence comes
this difference, if not in part from the difference

in foods, and difference in inheritance,* and in part
from the mixture of the diverse elements which
float around in the immensity of the void? The
mind, like the body, has its contagious diseases and
its scurvy.

Such is the influence of climate, that a man who
goes from one climate to another, feels the change,
in spite of himself. He is a walking plant which
has transplanted itself; if the climate is not the
same, it will surely either degenerate or improve.

Furthermore, we catch everything from those
with whom we come in contact; their gestures, their
accent, etc.; just as the eyelid is instinctively lowered
when a blow is foreseen, or as (for the same reason)
the body of the spectator mechanically imitates, in
spite of himself, all the motions of a good mimic.[18]

From what I have just said, it follows that a
brilliant man is his own best company, unless he
can find other company of the same sort. In the
society of the unintelligent, the mind grows rusty
for lack of exercise, as at tennis a ball that is
served badly is badly returned. I should prefer an
intelligent man without an education, if he were
still young enough, to a man badly educated. A
badly trained mind is like an actor whom the prov-
inces have spoiled.

Thus, the diverse states of the soul are always
correlative with those of the body.[19] But the better
to show this dependence, in its completeness and
its causes, let us here make use of comparative
anatomy; let us lay bare the organs of man and

* The history of animals and of men proves how the mind
and the body of children are dominated by their inheritance
from their fathers.

of animals. How can human nature be known, if we may not derive any light from an exact comparison of the structure of man and of animals?

In general, the form and the structure of the brains of quadrupeds are almost the same as those of the brain of man; the same shape, the same arrangement everywhere, with this essential difference, that of all the animals man is the one whose brain is largest, and, in proportion to its mass, more convoluted than the brain of any other animal; then come the monkey, the beaver, the elephant, the dog, the fox, the cat. These animals are most like man, for among them, too, one notes the same progressive analogy in relation to the *corpus callosum* in which Lancisi—anticipating the late M. de la Peyronie[20]—established the seat of the soul. The latter, however, illustrated the theory by innumerable experiments. Next after all the quadrupeds, birds have the largest brains. Fish have large heads, but these are void of sense, like the heads of many men. Fish have no *corpus callosum,* and very little brain, while insects entirely lack brain.

I shall not launch out into any more detail about the varieties of nature, nor into conjectures concerning them, for there is an infinite number of both, as any one can see by reading no further than the treatises of Willis "De Cerebro" and "De Anima Brutorum."[21]

I shall draw the conclusions which follow clearly from these incontestable observations: 1st, that the fiercer animals are, the less brain they have; 2d, that this organ seems to increase in size in proportion to the gentleness of the animal; 3d, that nature seems here eternally to impose a singular condition, that the more one gains in intelligence the more one loses in instinct. Does this bring gain or loss?

Do not think, however, that I wish to infer by that, that the size alone of the brain, is enough to indicate the degree of tameness in animals: the quality must correspond to the quantity, and the solids and liquids must be in that due equilibrium which constitutes health.

If, as is ordinarily observed, the imbecile does not lack brain, his brain will be deficient in its consistency—for instance, in being too soft. The same thing is true of the insane, and the defects of their brains do not always escape our investigation. But if the causes of imbecility, insanity, etc., are not obvious, where shall we look for the causes of the diversity of all minds? They would escape the eyes of a lynx and of an argus. A mere nothing, a tiny fibre, something that could never be found by the most delicate anatomy, would have made of Erasmus and Fontenelle[22] two idiots, and Fontenelle himself speaks of this very fact in one of his best dialogues.

Willis has noticed in addition to the softness of the brain-substance in children, puppies, and birds, that the *corpora striata* are obliterated and discolored in all these animals, and that the striations are as imperfectly formed as in paralytics.....

However cautious and reserved one may be about the consequences that can be deduced from these observations, and from many others concerning the kind of variation in the organs, nerves, etc., [one must admit that] so many different varieties can not be the gratuitous play of nature. They prove at least the necessity for a good and vigorous phys-

ical organization, since throughout the animal kingdom the soul gains force with the body and ac-
quires keenness, as the body gains strength.

Let us pause to contemplate the varying capacity
of animals to learn. Doubtless the analogy best
framed leads the mind to think that the causes we
have mentioned produce all the difference that is
found between animals and men, although we must
confess that our weak understanding, limited to the
coarsest observations, can not see the bonds that
exist between cause and effects. This is a kind of
harmony that philosophers will never know.

Among animals, some learn to speak and sing;
they remember tunes, and strike the notes as exactly as a musician. Others, for instance the ape,
show more intelligence, and yet can not learn music.
What is the reason for this, except some defect in
the organs of speech? But is this defect so essential to the structure that it could never be remedied?
In a word, would it be absolutely impossible to
teach the ape a language?[23] I do not think so.

I should choose a large ape in preference to any
other, until by some good fortune another kind
should be discovered, more like us, for nothing
prevents there being such an one in regions unknown to us. The ape resembles us so strongly
that naturalists have called it "wild man" or "man
of the woods." I should take it in the condition
of the pupils of Amman,[24] that is to say, I should
not want it to be too young or too old; for apes
that are brought to Europe are usually too old.
I would choose the one with the most intelligent
face, and the one which, in a thousand little ways,
best lived up to its look of intelligence. Finally

not considering myself worthy to be his master,
I should put him in the school of that excellent
teacher whom I have just named, or with another
teacher equally skilful, if there is one.

You know by Amman's work, and by all those*
who have interpreted his method, all the wonders
he has been able to accomplish for those born deaf.
In their eyes he discovered ears, as he himself ex-
plains, and in how short a time! In short he taught
them to hear, speak, read, and write. I grant that
a deaf person's eyes see more clearly and are keener
than if he were not deaf, for the loss of one member
or sense can increase the strength or acuteness of
another, but apes see and hear, they understand
what they hear and see, and grasp so perfectly the
signs that are made to them, that I doubt not that
they would surpass the pupils of Amman in any
other game or exercise. Why then should the education of monkeys be impossible? Why might not
the monkey, by dint of great pains, at last imitate
after the manner of deaf mutes, the motions necessary for pronunciation? I do not dare decide
whether the monkey's organs of speech, however
trained, would be incapable of articulation. But,
because of the great analogy between ape and man[25]
and because there is no known animal whose external and internal organs so strikingly resemble man's,
it would surprise me if speech were absolutely impossible to the ape. Locke, who was certainly
never suspected of credulity, found no difficulty
in believing the story told by Sir William Temple[26]
in his memoirs, about a parrot which could answer rationally, and which had learned to carry

* The author of "The Natural History of the Soul."

on a kind of connected conversation, as we do.
I know that people have ridiculed* this great meta-
physician; but suppose some one should have an-
nounced that reproduction sometimes takes place
without eggs or a female, would he have found
many partisans? Yet M. Trembley[27] has found
cases where reproduction takes place without copu-
lation and by fission. Would not Amman too have
passed for mad if he had boasted that he could
instruct scholars like his in so short a time, before
he had happily accomplished the feat? His suc-
cesses have, however, astonished the world; and
he, like the author of "The History of Polyps," has
risen to immortality at one bound. Whoever owes
the miracles that he works to his own genius sur-
passes, in my opinion, the man who owes his to
chance. He who has discovered the art of adorning
the most beautiful of the kingdoms [of nature], and
of giving it perfections that it did not have, should be
rated above an idle creator of frivolous systems, or a
painstaking author of sterile discoveries. Amman's
discoveries are certainly of a much greater value;
he has freed men from the instinct to which they
seemed to be condemned, and has given them ideas,
intelligence, or in a word, a soul which they would
never have had. What greater power than this!

Let us not limit the resources of nature; they
are infinite, especially when reinforced by great art.

Could not the device which opens the Eustachian
canal of the deaf, open that of apes? Might not a
happy desire to imitate the master's pronunciation,
liberate the organs of speech in animals that imitate
so many other signs with such skill and intelligence?

* The author of "The History of the Soul."

Not only do I defy any one to name any really conclusive experiment which proves my view impossible and absurd; but such is the likeness of the structure and functions of the ape to ours that I have very little doubt that if this animal were properly trained he might at last be taught to pronounce, and consequently to know, a language. Then he would no longer be a wild man, nor a defective man, but he would be a perfect man, a little gentleman, with as much matter or muscle as we have, for thinking and profiting by his education.

The transition from animals to man is not violent, as true philosophers will admit. What was man before the invention of words and the knowledge of language?[28] An animal of his own species with much less instinct than the others. In those days, he did not consider himself king over the other animals, nor was he distinguished from the ape, and from the rest, except as the ape itself differs from the other animals, i. e., by a more intelligent face. Reduced to the bare intuitive knowledge of the Leibnizians he saw only shapes and colors, without being able to distinguish between them: the same, old as young, child at all ages, he lisped out his sensations and his needs, as a dog that is hungry or tired of sleeping, asks for something to eat, or for a walk.

Words, languages, laws, sciences, and the fine arts have come, and by them finally the rough diamond of our mind has been polished. Man has been trained in the same way as animals. He has become an author, as they became beasts of burden. A geometrician has learned to perform the most difficult demonstrations and calculations, as a monkey has learned to take his little hat off and on, and to mount his tame dog. All has been accomplished through signs, every species has learned what it could understand, and in this way men have acquired symbolic knowledge, still so called by our German philosophers.

Nothing, as any one can see, is so simple as the mechanism of our education. Everything may be reduced to sounds or words that pass from the mouth of one through the ears of another into his brain. At the same moment, he perceives through his eyes the shape of the bodies of which these words are the arbitrary signs.

But who was the first to speak? Who was the first teacher of the human race? Who invented the means of utilizing the plasticity of our organism? I can not answer: the names of these first splendid geniuses have been lost in the night of time. But art is the child of nature, so nature must have long preceded it.

We must think that the men who were the most highly organized, those on whom nature had lavished her richest gifts, taught the others. They could not have heard a new sound for instance, nor experienced new sensations, nor been struck by all the varied and beautiful objects that compose the ravishing spectacle of nature without finding themselves in the state of mind of the deaf man of Chartres, whose experience was first related by the great Fontenelle,[29] when, at forty years, he heard for the first time, the astonishing sound of bells.

Would it be absurd to conclude from this that the first mortals tried after the manner of this deaf man, or like animals and like mutes (another kind of animals), to express their new feelings by motions depending on the nature of their imagination, and therefore afterwards by spontaneous sounds, distinctive of each animal, as the natural expression of their surprise, their joy, their ecstasies and their needs? For doubtless those whom nature endowed with finer feeling had also greater facility in expression.

That is the way in which, I think, men have used their feeling and their instinct to gain intelligence and then have employed their intelligence to gain knowledge. Those are the ways, so far as I can understand them, in which men have filled the brain with the ideas, for the reception of which nature made it. Nature and man have helped each other; and the smallest beginnings have, little by little, increased, until everything in the universe could be as easily described as a circle.

As a violin string or a harpsichord key vibrates and gives forth sound, so the cerebral fibres, struck by waves of sound, are stimulated to render or repeat the words that strike them. And as the structure of the brain is such that when eyes well formed for seeing, have once perceived the image of objects, the brain can not help seeing their images and their differences, so when the signs of these differences have been traced or imprinted in the brain, the soul necessarily examines their relations—an examination that would have been impossible without the discovery of signs or the invention of language. At the time when the universe was almost dumb, the soul's attitude toward all objects was that of a man without any idea of proportion toward a picture or a piece of sculpture, in which he could distinguish nothing; or the soul was like a little child (for the soul was then in its infancy) who, holding in his hand small bits of straw or wood, sees them in a vague and superficial way without being able to count or distinguish them.   But let some one attach a kind of banner, or standard, to this bit of wood (which perhaps is called a mast), and another banner to another similar object; let the first be known by the symbol 1, and the second by the symbol or number 2, then the child will be able to count the objects, and in this way he will learn all of arithmetic.   As soon as one figure seems equal to another in its numerical sign, he will decide without difficulty that they are two different bodies, that $1 + 1$ make 2, and $2 + 2$ make 4,* etc.

This real or apparent likeness of figures is the fundamental basis of all truths and of all we know. Among these sciences, evidently those whose signs are less simple and less sensible are harder to understand than the others, because more talent is required to comprehend and combine the immense number of words by which such sciences express the truths in their province.   On the other hand, the sciences that are expressed by numbers or by other small signs, are easily learned; and without doubt this facility rather than its demonstrability is what has made the fortune of algebra.

All this knowledge, with which vanity fills the balloon-like brains of our proud pedants, is therefore but a huge mass of words and figures, which form in the brain all the marks by which we dis-

---

* There are peoples, even to-day, who, through lack of a greater number of signs, can count only to 20.

tinguish and recall objects. All our ideas are awakened after the fashion in which the gardener who
knows plants recalls all stages of their growth at
sight of them. These words and the objects desig-
nated by them are so connected in the brain that it is
comparatively rare to imagine a thing without the
name or sign that is attached to it.

I always use the word "imagine," because I think
that everything is the work of imagination, and
that all the faculties of the soul can be correctly
reduced to pure imagination in which they all consist.[30] Thus judgment, reason, and memory are
not absolute parts of the soul, but merely modifications of this kind of medullary screen upon
which images of the objects painted in the eye are
projected as by a magic lantern.

But if such is the marvelous and incomprehensible result of the structure of the brain, if everything is perceived and explained by imagination,
why should we divide the sensitive principle which
thinks in man? Is not this a clear inconsistency
in the partisans of the simplicity of the mind?
For a thing that is divided can no longer without
absurdity be regarded as indivisible. See to what
one is brought by the abuse of language and by
those fine words (spirituality, immateriality, etc.)
used haphazard and not understood even by the
most brilliant.[31]

Nothing is easier than to prove a system based, as
this one is, on the intimate feeling and personal
experience of each individual. If the imagination,
or, let us say, that fantastic part of the brain whose
nature is as unknown to us as its way of acting, be
naturally small or weak, it will hardly be able to

compare the analogy or the resemblance of its ideas,
it will be able to see only what is face to face with
it, or what affects it very strongly; and how will
it see all this! Yet it is always imagination which
apperceives, and imagination which represents to
itself all objects along with their names and sym-
bols; and thus, once again, imagination is the soul,
since it plays all the rôles of the soul. By the imagination, by its flattering brush, the cold skeleton
of reason takes on living and ruddy flesh, by the
imagination the sciences flourish, the arts are
adorned, the wood speaks, the echoes sigh, the
rocks weep, marble breathes, and all inanimate objects gain life. It is imagination again which adds
the piquant charm of voluptuousness to the tenderness of an amorous heart; which makes tenderness
bud in the study of the philosopher and of the
dusty pedant, which, in a word, creates scholars as
well as orators and poets. Foolishly decried by
some, vainly praised by others, and misunderstood
by all; it follows not only in the train of the graces
and of the fine arts, it not only describes, but can
also measure nature. It reasons, judges, analyzes,
compares, and investigates. Could it feel so keenly
the beauties of the pictures drawn for it, unless it
discovered their relations? No, just as it can not
turn its thoughts on the pleasures of the senses,
without enjoying their perfection or their voluptuousness, it can not reflect on what it has mechanically conceived, without thus being judgment itself.

The more the imagination or the poorest talent
is exercised, the more it gains in *embonpoint*, so to
speak, and the larger it grows. It becomes sensi-

tive, robust, broad, and capable of thinking. The best of organisms has need of this exercise.

Man's preeminent advantage is his organism.[32] In vain all writers of books on morals fail to regard as praiseworthy those qualities that come by nature, esteeming only the talents gained by dint of reflection and industry. For whence come, I ask, skill, learning, and virtue, if not from a disposition that makes us fit to become skilful, wise and virtuous? And whence again, comes this disposition, if not from nature? Only through nature do we have any good qualities; to her we owe all that we are. Why then should I not esteem men with good natural qualities as much as men who shine by acquired and as it were borrowed virtues? Whatever the virtue may be, from whatever source it may come, it is worthy of esteem; the only question is, how to estimate it. Mind, beauty, wealth, nobility, although the children of chance, all have their own value, as skill, learning and virtue have theirs. Those upon whom nature has heaped her most costly gifts should pity those to whom these gifts have been refused; but, in their character of experts, they may feel their superiority without pride. A beautiful woman would be as foolish to think herself ugly, as an intelligent man to think himself a fool. An exaggerated modesty (a rare fault, to be sure) is a kind of ingratitude towards nature. An honest pride, on the contrary, is the mark of a strong and beautiful soul, revealed by manly features moulded by feeling.

If one's organism is an advantage, and the preeminent advantage, and the source of all others, education is the second. The best made brain would

be a total loss without it, just as the best con-
stituted man would be but a common peasant, without knowledge of the ways of the world. But, on
the other hand, what would be the use of the most
excellent school, without a matrix perfectly open
to the entrance and conception of ideas? It is
.... impossible to impart a single idea to a man
deprived of all his senses.....

But if the brain is at the same time well organized
and well educated, it is a fertile soil, well sown,
that brings forth a hundredfold what it has received: or (to leave the figures of speech often
needed to express what one means, and to add grace
to truth itself) the imagination, raised by art to the
rare and beautiful dignity of genius, apprehends
exactly all the relations of the ideas it has conceived, and takes in easily an astounding number of
objects, in order to deduce from them a long chain
of consequences, which are again but new relations,
produced by a comparison with the first, to which
the soul finds a perfect resemblance. Such is, I
think, the generation of intelligence.[33] I say "finds"
as I before gave the epithet "apparent" to the
likeness of objects, not because I think that our
senses are always deceivers, as Father Malebranche
has claimed, or that our eyes, naturally a little un-
steady, fail to see objects as they are in themselves,
(though microscopes prove this to us every day) but
in order to avoid any dispute with the Pyrrhon-
ians,[34] among whom Bayle[35] is well known.

I say of truth in general what M. de Fontenelle
says of certain truths in particular, that we must
sacrifice it in order to remain on good terms with
society. And it accords with the gentleness of my

character, to avoid all disputes unless to whet conversation. The Cartesians would here in vain make an onset upon me with their innate ideas. I certainly would not give myself a quarter of the trouble that M. Locke took, to attack such chimeras. In truth, what is the use of writing a ponderous volume to prove a doctrine which became an axiom three thousand years ago?

According to the principles which we have laid down, and which we consider true; he who has the most imagination should be regarded as having the most intelligence or genius, for all these words are synonymous; and again, only by a shameful abuse [of terms] do we think that we are saying different things, when we are merely using different words, different sounds, to which no idea or real distinction is attached.

The finest, greatest, or strongest imagination is then the one most suited to the sciences as well as to the arts. I do not pretend to say whether more intellect is necessary to excel in the art of Aristotle or of Descartes than to excel in that of Euripides or of Sophocles, and whether nature has taken more trouble to make Newton than to make Corneille, though I doubt this. But it is certain that imagination alone, differently applied, has produced their diverse triumphs and their immortal glory.

If one is known as having little judgment and much imagination, this means that the imagination has been left too much alone, has, as it were, occupied most of the time in looking at itself in the mirror of its sensations, has not sufficiently formed the habit of examining the sensations themselves attentively. [It means that the imagination] has been more impressed by images than by their truth or their likeness.

Truly, so quick are the responses of the imagination that if attention, that key or mother of the sciences, does not do its part, imagination can do little more than run over and skim its objects.

See that bird on the bough: it seems always ready to fly away. Imagination is like the bird, always carried onward by the turmoil of the blood and the animal spirits. One wave leaves a mark, effaced by the one that follows; the soul pursues it, often in vain: it must expect to regret the loss of that which it has not quickly enough seized and fixed. Thus, imagination, the true image of time, is being ceaselessly destroyed and renewed.

Such is the chaos and the continuous quick succession of our ideas: they drive each other away even as one wave yields to another. Therefore, if imagination does not, as it were, use one set of its muscles to maintain a kind of equilibrium with the fibres of the brain, to keep its attention for a while upon an object that is on the point of disappearing, and to prevent itself from contemplating prematurely another object—[unless the imagination does all this], it will never be worthy of the fine name of judgment. It will express vividly what it has perceived in the same fashion: it will create orators, musicians, painters, poets, but never a single philosopher. On the contrary, if the imagination be trained from childhood to bridle itself and to keep from being carried away by its own impetuosity— an impetuosity which creates only brilliant enthusiasts—and to check, to restrain, its ideas, to exam-

ine them in all their aspects in order to see all sides
of an object, then the imagination, ready in judgment, will comprehend the greatest possible sphere
of objects, through reasoning; and its vivacity (always so good a sign in children, and only needing
to be regulated by study and training) will be only
a far-seeing insight without which little progress
can be made in the sciences.

Such are the simple foundations upon which the
edifice of logic has been reared. Nature has built
these foundations for the whole human race, but
some have used them, while others have abused
them.

In spite of all these advantages of man over animals, it is doing him honor to place him in the
same class. For, truly, up to a certain age, he is
more of an animal than they, since at birth he has
less instinct. What animal would die of hunger in
the midst of a river of milk? Man alone. Like
that child of olden time to whom a modern writer,
refers, following Arnobius,[36] he knows neither the
foods suitable for him, nor the water that can
drown him, nor the fire that can reduce him to
ashes. Light a wax candle for the first time under
a child's eyes, and he will mechanically put his
fingers in the flame as if to find out what is the
new thing that he sees. It is at his own cost that
he will learn of the danger, but he will not be caught
again. Or, put the child with an animal on a precipice, the child alone falls off; he drowns where
the animal would save itself by swimming. At four-
teen or fifteen years the child knows hardly anything
of the great pleasures in store for him, in the reproduction of his species; when he is a youth, he

does not know exactly how to behave in a game
which nature teaches animals so quickly. He hides
himself as if he were ashamed of taking pleasure,
and of having been made to be happy, while animals
frankly glory in being cynics. Without education,
they are without prejudices. For one more example, let us observe a dog and a child who have
lost their master on a highway: the child cries
and does not know to what saint to pray, while the
dog, better helped by his sense of smell than the
child by his reason, soon finds his master.

Thus nature made us to be lower than animals
or at least to exhibit all the more, because of that
native inferiority, the wonderful efficacy of education which alone raises us from the level of the
animals and lifts us above them. But shall we grant
this same distinction to the deaf and to the blind,
to imbeciles, madmen, or savages, or to those who
have been brought up in the woods with animals;
to those who have lost their imagination through
melancholia, or in short to all those animals in
human form who give evidence of only the rudest
instinct? No, all these, men of body but not of
mind, do not deserve to be classed by themselves.

We do not intend to hide from ourselves the
arguments that can be brought forward against our
belief and in favor of a primitive distinction between
men and animals. Some say that there is in man
a natural law, a knowledge of good and evil, which
has never been imprinted on the heart of animals.

But is this objection, or rather this assertion, based
on observation? Any assertion unfounded on observation may be rejected by a philosopher. Have
we ever had a single experience which convinces

us that man alone has been enlightened by a ray
denied all other animals? If there is no such experience, we can no more know what goes on in animals' minds or even in the minds of other men,
than we can help feeling what affects the inner part
of our own being. We know that we think, and
feel remorse—an intimate feeling forces us to recognize this only too well; but this feeling in us is
insufficient to enable us to judge the remorse of
others. That is why we have to take others at
their word, or judge them by the sensible and external signs we have noticed in ourselves when we
experienced the same accusations of conscience and
the same torments.

In order to decide whether animals which do not
talk have received the natural law, we must, therefore, have recourse to those signs to which I have
just referred, if any such exist. The facts seem to
prove it. A dog that bit the master who was teas-
ing it, seemed to repent a minute afterwards; it
looked sad, ashamed, afraid to show itself, and
seemed to confess its guilt by a crouching and
downcast air. History offers us a famous example
of a lion which would not devour a man abandoned
to its fury, because it recognized him as its bene-
factor. How much might it be wished that man
himself always showed the same gratitude for kind-
nesses, and the same respect for humanity! Then
we should no longer fear either ungrateful wretches,
or wars which are the plague of the human race
and the real executioners of the natural law.

But a being to which nature has given such a
precocious and enlightened instinct, which judges,
combines, reasons, and deliberates as far as the

sphere of its activity extends and permits, a being which feels attachment because of benefits received, and which leaving a master who treats it badly goes to seek a better one, a being with a structure like ours, which performs the same acts, has the same passions, the same griefs, the same pleasures, more or less intense according to the sway of the imagination and the delicacy of the nervous organization— does not such a being show clearly that it knows its faults and ours, understands good and evil, and in a word, has consciousness of what it does? Would its soul, which feels the same joys, the same mortification and the same discomfiture which we feel, remain utterly unmoved by disgust when it saw a fellow-creature torn to bits, or when it had itself pitilessly dismembered this fellow-creature? If this be granted, it follows that the precious gift now in question would not have been denied to animals: for since they show us sure signs of repentance, as well as of intelligence, what is there absurd in thinking that beings, almost as perfect machines as ourselves, are, like us, made to understand and to feel nature?

Let no one object that animals, for the most part, are savage beasts, incapable of realizing the evil that they do; for do all men discriminate better between vice and virtue? There is ferocity in our species as well as in theirs. Men who are in the barbarous habit of breaking the natural law are not tormented as much by it, as those who transgress it for the first time, and who have not been hardened by the force of habit. The same thing is true of animals as of men—both may be more or less ferocious in temperament, and both become more so by living with others like themselves. But a gentle and peaceful animal which lives among other animals of the same disposition and of gentle nurture, will be an enemy of blood and carnage; it will blush internally at having shed blood. There is perhaps this difference, that since among animals everything is sacrificed to their needs, to their pleasures, to the necessities of life, which they enjoy more than we, their remorse apparently should not be as keen as ours, because we are not in the same state of necessity as they. Custom perhaps dulls and perhaps stifles remorse as well as pleasures.

But I will suppose for a moment that I am utterly mistaken in concluding that almost all the world holds a wrong opinion on this subject, while I alone am right. I will grant that animals, even the best of them, do not know the difference between moral good and evil, that they have no recollection of the trouble taken for them, of the kindness done them, no realization of their own virtues. [I will suppose], for instance, that this lion, to which I, like so many others, have referred, does not remember at all that it refused to kill the man, abandoned to its fury, in a combat more inhuman than one could find among lions, tigers and bears, put together. For our compatriots fight, Swiss against Swiss, brother against brother, recognize each other, and yet capture and kill each other without remorse, because a prince pays for the murder. I suppose in short that the natural law has not been given animals. What will be the consequences of this supposition? Man is not moulded from a costlier clay; nature has used but one dough, and has merely varied the leaven. Therefore if animals do not repent for having vio-

lated this inmost feeling which I am discussing, or
rather if they absolutely lack it, man must necessarily be in the same condition.   Farewell then to
the natural law and all the fine treatises published
about it! The whole animal kingdom in general
would be deprived of it. But, conversely, if man can
not dispense with the belief that when health permits
him to be himself, he always distinguishes the upright, humane, and virtuous, from those who are not
humane, virtuous, nor honorable: that it is easy
to tell vice from virtue, by the unique pleasure and
the peculiar repugnance that seem to be their natural
effects, it follows that animals, composed of the
same matter, lacking perhaps only one degree of
fermentation to make it exactly like man's, must
share the same prerogatives of animal nature, and
that thus there exists no soul or sensitive substance
without remorse.[37]   The following consideration
will reinforce these observations.

It is impossible to destroy the natural law. The
impress of it on all animals is so strong, that I have
no doubt that the wildest and most savage have
some moments of repentance. I believe that that
cruel maid of Chalons in Champagne must have
sorrowed for her crime, if she really ate her sister.
I think that the same thing is true of all those who
commit crimes, even involuntary or temperamental
crimes: true of Gaston of Orleans who could not
help stealing; of a certain woman who was subject
to the same crime when pregnant, and whose children inherited it; of the woman who, in the same
condition, ate her husband; of that other woman
who killed her children, salted their bodies, and ate
a piece of them every day, as a little relish; of that

daughter of a thief and cannibal who at twelve
years followed in his steps, although she had been
orphaned when she was a year old, and had been
brought up by honest people; to say nothing of
many other examples of which the records of our
observers are full, all of them proving that there
are a thousand hereditary vices and virtues which
are transmitted from parents to children as those
of the foster mother pass to the children she nurses.
Now, I believe and admit that these wretches do
not for the most part feel at the time the enormity
of their actions. Bulimia, or canine hunger, for example, can stifle all feeling; it is a mania of the
stomach that one is compelled to satisfy, but what
remorse must be in store for those women, when
they come to themselves and grow sober, and remember the crimes they have committed against those
they held most dear! What a punishment for an
involuntary crime which they could not resist, of
which they had no consciousness whatever! However, this is apparently not enough for the judges.
For of these women, of whom I tell, one was cruelly
beaten and burned, and another was buried alive.
I realize all that is demanded by the interest of society. But doubtless it is much to be wished that
excellent physicians might be the only judges. They
alone could tell the innocent criminal from the
guilty. If reason is the slave of a depraved or mad
desire, how can it control the desire?

But if crime carries with it its own more or less
cruel punishment, if the most continued and most
barbarous habit can not entirely blot out repentance in the cruelest hearts, if criminals are lacerated
by the very memory of their deeds, why should we

frighten the imagination of weak minds, by a hell,
by specters, and by precipices of fire even less real
than those of Pascal?* Why must we have recourse
to fables, as an honest pope once said himself, to
torment even the unhappy wretches who are executed, because we do not think that they are sufficiently punished by their own conscience, their first
executioner? I do not mean to say that all criminals are unjustly punished; I only maintain that
those whose will is depraved, and whose conscience
is extinguished, are punished enough by their remorse when they come to themselves, a remorse,
I venture to assert, from which nature should in
this case have delivered unhappy souls dragged on
by a fatal necessity.

Criminals, scoundrels, ingrates, those in short
without natural feelings, unhappy tyrants who are
unworthy of life, in vain take a cruel pleasure in
their barbarity, for there are calm moments of reflection in which the avenging conscience arises,
testifies against them, and condemns them to be
almost ceaselessly torn to pieces at their own hands.
Whoever torments men is tormented by himself;
and the sufferings that he will experience will be
the just measure of those that he has inflicted.

On the other hand, there is so much pleasure in

---

* In a company, or at table, he always required a rampart
of chairs or else some one close to him at the left, to prevent
his seeing horrible abysses into which (in spite of his understanding these illusions) he sometimes feared that he might
fall. What a frightful result of imagination, or of the peculiar circulation in a lobe of the brain! Great man on one side of
his nature, on the other he was half-mad. Madness and wisdom,
each had its compartment, or its lobe, the two separated by
a fissure. Which was the side by which he was so strongly
attached to Messieurs of Port Royal? (I have read this in an
extract from the treatise on vertigo by M. de la Mettrie.)

doing good, in recognizing and appreciating what one receives, so much satisfaction in practising virtue, in being gentle, humane, kind, charitable, compassionate and generous (for this one word includes all the virtues), that I consider as sufficiently punished any one who is unfortunate enough not to have been born virtuous.

We were not originally made to be learned; we have become so perhaps by a sort of abuse of our organic faculties, and at the expense of the State which nourishes a host of sluggards whom vanity has adorned with the name of philosophers. Nature has created us all solely to be happy[38]—yes, all of us from the crawling worm to the eagle lost in the cloulds. For this cause she has given all animals some share of natural law, a share greater or less according to the needs of each animal's organs when in normal condition.

Now how shall we define natural law? It is a feeling that teaches us what we should not do, because we would not wish it to be done to us. Should I dare add to this common idea, that this feeling seems to me but a kind of fear or dread, as salutary to the race as to the individual; for may it not be true that we respect the purse and life of others only to save our own possessions, our honor, and ourselves; like those Ixions of Christianity[39] who love God and embrace so many fantastic virtues, merely because they are afraid of hell!

You see that natural law is but an intimate feeling that, like all other feelings (thought included), belongs also to imagination. Evidently, therefore, natural law does not presuppose education, revelation, nor legislator,—provided one does not propose to confuse natural law with civil laws, in the ridiculous fashion of the theologians.

The arms of fanaticism may destroy those who support these truths, but they will never destroy the truths themselves.

I do not mean to call in question the existence of a supreme being; on the contrary it seems to me that the greatest degree of probability is in favor of this belief. But since the existence of this being goes no further than that of any other toward proving the need of worship, it is a theoretic truth with very little practical value. Therefore, since we may say, after such long experience, that religion does not imply exact honesty, we are authorized by the same reasons to think that atheism does not exclude it.

Furthermore, who can be sure that the reason for man's existence is not simply the fact that he exists?[40] Perhaps he was thrown by chance on some spot on the earth's surface, nobody knows how nor why, but simply that he must live and die, like the mushrooms which appear from day to day, or like those flowers which border the ditches and cover the walls.

Let us not lose ourselves in the infinite, for we are not made to have the least idea thereof, and are absolutely unable to get back to the origin of things. Besides it does not matter for our peace of mind, whether matter be eternal or have been created, whether there be or be not a God. How foolish to torment ourselves so much about things which we can not know, and which would not make us any happier even were we to gain knowledge about them!

But, some will say, read all such works as those
of Fénelon,[41] of Nieuwentyt,[42] of Abadie,[43] of
Derham,[44] of Rais,[45] and the rest. Well! what will
they teach me or rather what have they taught
me? They are only tiresome repetitions of zealous
writers, one of whom adds to the other only verbiage, more likely to strengthen than to undermine
the foundations of atheism. The number of the
evidences drawn from the spectacle of nature does
not give these evidences any more force. Either
the mere structure of a finger, of an ear, of an eye,
a single observation of Malpighi[46] proves all, and
doubtless much better than Descartes and Malebranche proved it, or all the other evidences prove
nothing. Deists,[47] and even Christians, should therefore be content to point out that throughout the
animal kingdom the same aims are pursued and
accomplished by an infinite number of different
mechanisms, all of them however exactly geomet-
rical. For what stronger weapons could there be
with which to overthrow atheists? It is true that if
my reason does not deceive me, man and the whole
universe seem to have been designed for this unity
of aim. The sun, air, water, the organism, the
shape of bodies,—everything is brought to a focus
in the eye as in a mirror that faithfully presents
to the imagination all the objects reflected in it, in
accordance with the laws required by the infinite
variety of bodies which take part in vision. In ears
we find everywhere a striking variety, and yet the
difference of structure in men, animals, birds, and
fishes, does not produce different uses. All ears are
so mathematically made, that they tend equally to
one and the same end, namely, hearing. But would

Chance, the deist asks, be a great enough geometrician to vary thus, at pleasure, the works of which she is supposed to be the author, without being hindered by so great a diversity from gaining the same end? Again, the deist will bring forward as a difficulty those parts of the animal that are clearly contained in it for future use, the butterfly in the caterpillar, man in the sperm, a whole polyp in each of its parts, the valvule in the oval orifice, the lungs in the foetus, the teeth in their sockets, the bones in the fluid from which they detach themselves and (in an incomprehensible manner) harden. And since the partisans of this theory, far from neglecting anything that would strengthen it, never tire of piling up proof upon proof, they are willing to avail themselves of everything, even of the weakness of the mind in certain cases. Look, they say, at men like Spinoza, Vanini,[48] Desbarreau,[49] and Boindin,[50] apostles who honor deism more than they harm it. The duration of their health was the measure of their unbelief, and one rarely fails, they add, to renounce atheism when the passions, with their instrument, the body, have grown weak.

That is certainly the most that can be said in favor of the existence of God : although the last argument is frivolous in that these conversions are short, and the mind almost always regains its former opinions and acts accordingly, as soon as it has regained or rather rediscovered its strength in that of the body. That is, at least, much more than was said by the physician Diderot,[51] in his "Pensées Philosophiques," a sublime work that will not convince a single atheist. What reply can, in truth, be

made to a man who says, "We do not know nature;
causes hidden in her breast might have produced
everything. In your turn, observe the polyp of Trembley:[52] does it not contain in itself the causes which
bring about regeneration? Why then would it
be absurd to think that there are physical causes
by reason of which everything has been made, and
to which the whole chain of this vast universe is
so necessarily bound and held that nothing which
happens, could have failed to happen,[53]—causes,
of which we are so invincibly ignorant that we
have had recourse to a God, who, as some aver,
is not so much as a logical entity? Thus to destroy chance is not to prove the existence of a
supreme being, since there may be some other thing
which is neither chance nor God—I mean, nature.
It follows that the study of nature can make only
unbelievers; and the way of thinking of all its more
successful investigators proves this."

The weight of the universe therefore far from
crushing a real atheist does not even shake him.
All these evidences of a creator, repeated thousands
and thousands of times, evidences that are placed
far above the comprehension of men like us, are
self-evident (however far one push the argument)
only to the anti-Pyrrhonians,[54] or to those who
have enough confidence in their reason to believe
themselves capable of judging on the basis of certain phenomena, against which, as you see, the atheists can urge others perhaps equally strong and absolutely opposed. For if we listen to the naturalists
again, they will tell us that the very causes which,
in a chemist's hands, by a chance combination, made
the first mirror, in the hands of nature made the

pure water, the mirror of the simple shepherdess; that the motion which keeps the world going could have created it, that each body has taken the place assigned to it by its own nature, that the air must have surrounded the earth, and that iron and the other metals are produced by internal motions of the earth, for one and the same reason; that the sun is as much a natural product as electricity, that it was not made to warm the earth and its inhabitants, whom it sometimes burns, any more than the rain was made to make the seeds grow, which it often spoils; that the mirror and the water were no more made for people to see themselves in, than were all other polished bodies with this same property; that the eye is in truth a kind of glass in which the soul can contemplate the image of objects as they are presented to it by these bodies, but that it is not proved that this organ was really made expressly for this contemplation, nor purposely placed in its socket, and in short that it may well be that Lucretius,[55] the physician Lamy,[56] and all Epicureans both ancient and modern were right when they suggested that the eye sees only because it is formed and placed as it is,[57] and that, given once for all, the same rules of motion followed by nature in the generation and development of bodies, this marvelous organ could not have been formed and placed differently.

Such is the *pro* and the *con*, and the summary of those fine arguments that will eternally divide the philosophers. I do not take either side.

"Non nostrum inter vos tantas componere lites."[58]

This is what I said to one of my friends, a French-

man, as frank a Pyrronian as I, a man of much merit,
and worthy of a better fate. He gave me a very
singular answer in regard to the matter. "It is
true," he told me, "that the *pro* and *con* should not
disturb at all the soul of a philosopher, who sees
that nothing is proved with clearness enough to
force his consent, and that the arguments offered
on one side are neutralized by those of the other.
However," he continued, "the universe will never
be happy, unless it is atheistic."[59] Here are this
wretch's reasons. If atheism, said he, were generally accepted, all the forms of religion would then
be destroyed and cut off at the roots. No more
theological wars, no more soldiers of religion—such
terrible soldiers! Nature infected with a sacred
poison, would regain its rights and its purity. Deaf
to all other voices, tranquil mortals would follow
only the spontaneous dictates of their own being
the only commands which can never be despised
with impunity and which alone can lead us to happiness through the pleasant paths of virtue.

Such is natural law: whoever rigidly observes
it is a good man and deserves the confidence of
all the human race. Whoever fails to follow it
scrupulously affects, in vain, the specious exterior
of another religion; he is a scamp or a hypocrite
whom I distrust.

After this, let a vain people think otherwise, let
them dare affirm that even probity is at stake in
not believing in revelation, in a word that another
religion than that of nature is necessary, whatever
it may be. Such an assertion is wretched and pitiable; and so is the good opinion which each one
gives us of the religion he has embraced! We do

not seek here the votes of the crowd. Whoever
raises in his heart altars to superstition, is born to
worship idols and not to thrill to virtue.

But since all the faculties of the soul depend to
such a degree on the proper organization of the
brain and of the whole body, that apparently they
are but this organization itself, the soul is clearly
an enlightened machine. For finally, even if man
alone had received a share of natural law, would
he be any less a machine for that? A few more
wheels, a few more springs than in the most perfect
animals, the brain proportionally nearer the heart
and for this very reason receiving more blood—
any one of a number of unknown causes might always produce this delicate conscience so easily
wounded, this remorse which is no more foreign to
matter than to thought, and in a word all the differences that are supposed to exist here. Could the
organism then suffice for everything? Once more.
yes; since thought visibly develops with our organs,
why should not the matter of which they are composed be susceptible of remorse also, when once it
has acquired, with time, the faculty of feeling?

The soul is therefore but an empty word, of
which no one has any idea, and which an enlightened
man should use only to signify the part in us
that thinks.[60] Given the least principle of motion,
animated bodies will have all that is necessary for
moving, feeling, thinking, repenting, or in a word
for conducting themselves in the physical realm,
and in the moral realm which depends upon it.

Yet we take nothing for granted; those who perhaps think that all the difficulties have not yet been

removed shall now read of experiments that will completely satisfy them.

1. The flesh of all animals palpitates after death. This palpitation continues longer, the more cold blooded the animal is and the less it perspires. Tortoises, lizards, serpents, etc. are evidence of this.

2. Muscles separated from the body contract when they are stimulated.

3. The intestines keep up their peristaltic or vermicular motion for a long time.

4. According to Cowper,[61] a simple injection of hot water reanimates the heart and the muscles.

5. A frog's heart moves for an hour or more after it has been removed from the body, especially when exposed to the sun or better still when placed on a hot table or chair. If this movement seems totally lost, one has only to stimulate the heart, and that hollow muscle beats again. Harvey[62] made this same observation on toads.

6. Bacon of Verulam[63] in his treatise "Sylva Sylvarum" cites the case of a man convicted of treason, who was opened alive, and whose heart thrown into hot water leaped several times, each time less high, to the perpendicular height of two feet.

7. Take a tiny chicken still in the egg, cut out the heart and you will observe the same phenomena as before, under almost the same conditions. The warmth of the breath alone reanimates an animal about to perish in the air pump.

The same experiments, which we owe to Boyle[64] and to Stenon,[65] are made on pigeons, dogs, and rabbits. Pieces of their hearts beat as their whole hearts would. The same movements can be seen in paws that have been cut off from moles.

8. The caterpillar, the worm, the spider, the fly, the eel — all exhibit the same phenomena; and in hot water, because of the fire it contains, the movement of the detached parts increases.

9. A drunken soldier cut off with one stroke of his sabre an Indian rooster's head. The animal remained standing, then walked, and ran: happening to run against a wall, it turned around, beat its wings still running, and finally fell down. As it lay on the ground, all the muscles of this rooster kept on moving. That is what I saw myself, and almost the same phenomena can easily be observed in kittens or puppies with their heads cut off.

10. Polyps do more than move after they have been cut in pieces. In a week they regenerate to form as many animals as there are pieces. I am sorry that these facts speak against the naturalists' system of generation; or rather I am very glad of it, for let this discovery teach us never to reach a general conclusion even on the ground of all known (and most decisive) experiments.

Here we have many more facts than are needed to prove, in an incontestable way, that each tiny fibre or part of an organized body moves by a principle which belongs to it. Its activity, unlike voluntary motions, does not depend in any way on the nerves, since the movements in question occur in parts of the body which have no connection with the circulation. But if this force is manifested even in sections of fibres the heart, which is a composite of peculiarly connected fibres, must possess the same property. I did not need Bacon's story to persuade

me of this. It was easy for me to come to this conclusion, both from the perfect analogy of the structure of the human heart with that of animals, and
also from the very bulk of the human heart, in which
this movement escapes our eyes only because it is
smothered, and finally because in corpses all the
organs are cold and lifeless. If executed criminals
were dissected while their bodies are still warm, we
should probably see in their hearts the same movements that are observed in the face-muscles of those
that have been beheaded.

The motive principle of the whole body, and even
of its parts cut in pieces, is such that it produces
not irregular movements, as some have thought,
but very regular ones, in warm blooded and perfect
animals as well as in cold and imperfect ones. No
resource therefore remains open to our adversaries
but to deny thousands and thousands of facts which
every man can easily verify.

If now any one ask me where is this innate force
in our bodies, I answer that it very clearly resides
in what the ancients called the parenchyma, that is
to say, in the very substance of the organs not including the veins, the arteries, the nerves, in a
word, that it resides in the organization of the
whole body, and that consequently each organ contains within itself forces more or less active according to the need of them.

Let us now go into some detail concerning these
springs of the human machine. All the vital, animal, natural, and automatic motions are carried on
by their action. Is it not in a purely mechanical
way that the body shrinks back when it is struck
with terror at the sight of an unforeseen precipice,

that the eyelids are lowered at the menace of a blow, as some have remarked, and that the pupil contracts in broad daylight to save the retina, and dilates to see objects in darkness? Is it not by mechanical means that the pores of the skin close in winter so that the cold can not penetrate to the interior of the blood vessels, and that the stomach vomits when it is irritated by poison, by a certain quantity of opium and by all emetics, etc.? that the heart, the arteries and the muscles contract in sleep as well as in waking hours, that the lungs serve as bellows continually in exercise,....that the heart contracts more strongly than any other muscle?[66]...

I shall not go into any more detail concerning all these little subordinate forces, well known to all. But there is another more subtle and marvelous force, which animates them all; it is the source of all our feelings, of all our pleasures, of all our passions, and of all our thoughts: for the brain has its muscles for thinking, as the legs have muscles for walking.[67] I wish to speak of this impetuous principle that Hippocrates calls ἐνορμῶν (soul). This principle exists and has its seat in the brain at the origin of the nerves, by which it exercises its control over all the rest of the body. By this fact is explained all that can be explained, even to the surprising effects of maladies of the imagination.....

Look at the portrait of the famous Pope who is, to say the least, the Voltaire of the English. The effort, the energy of his genius are imprinted upon his countenance. It is convulsed. His eyes protrude from their sockets, the eyebrows are raised with the muscles of the forehead. Why? Because the brain is in travail and all the body must share

in such a laborious deliverance. If there were not
an internal cord which pulled the external ones,
whence would come all these phenomena? To admit
a soul as explanation of them, is to be reduced to
[explaining phenomena by] the operations of the
Holy Spirit.

In fact, if what thinks in my brain is not a part
of this organ and therefore of the whole body, why
does my blood boil, and the fever of my mind pass
into my veins, when lying quietly in bed, I am forming the plan of some work or carrying on an abstract calculation? Put this question to men of imagination, to great poets, to men who are enraptured
by the felicitous expression of sentiment, and trans-
ported by an exquisite fancy or by the charms of
nature, of truth, or of virtue! By their enthusiasm,
by what they will tell you they have experienced,
you will judge the cause by its effects; by that harmony which Borelli,[68] a mere anatomist, understood
better than all the Leibnizians, you will comprehend
the material unity of man. In short, if the nerve-
tension which causes pain occasions also the fever
by which the distracted mind loses its will-power,
and if, conversely, the mind too much excited, disturbs the body (and kindles that inner fire which
killed Bayle while he was still so young); if an
agitation rouses my desire and my ardent wish for
what, a moment ago, I cared nothing about, and if
in their turn certain brain impressions excite the
same longing and the same desires, then why should
we regard as double what is manifestly one being?
In vain you fall back on the power of the will, since
for one order that the will gives, it bows a hundred
times to the yoke.[69] And what wonder that in

health the body obeys, since a torrent of blood
and of animal spirits[70] forces its obedience, and
since the will has as ministers an invisible legion of
fluids swifter than lightning and ever ready to do
its bidding! But as the power of the will is exercised by means of the nerves, it is likewise limited
by them.....

Does the result of jaundice surprise you? Do
you not know that the color of bodies depends on
the color of the glasses through which we look at
them,[71] and that whatever is the color of the humors,
such is the color of objects, at least for us, vain
playthings of a thousand illusions? But remove
this color from the aqueous humor of the eye, let
the bile flow through its natural filter, then the soul
having new eyes, will no longer see yellow. Again, is
it not thus, by removing cataract, or by injecting the
Eustachian canal, that sight is restored to the blind,
or hearing to the deaf? How many people, who
were perhaps only clever charlatans, passed for mir-
acle workers in the dark ages! Beautiful the soul,
and powerful the will which can not act save by
permission of the bodily conditions, and whose
tastes change with age and fever! Should we, then,
be astonished that philosophers have always had
in mind the health of the body, to preserve the
health of the soul, that Pythagoras[72] gave rules for
the diet as carefully as Plato forbade wine?[73] The
regime suited to the body is always the one with
which sane physicians think they must begin, when
it is a question of forming the mind, and of instruct-
ing it in the knowledge of truth and virtue; but these
are vain words in the disorder of illness, and in the
tumult of the senses. Without the precepts of hy-

giene, Epictetus, Socrates, Plato, and the rest
preach in vain: all ethics is fruitless for one who
lacks his share of temperance; it is the source of
all virtues, as intemperance is the source of all
vices.

Is more needed, (for why lose myself in dis-
cussion of the passions which are all explained by
the term, ἐνορμῶν, of Hippocrates) to prove that man
is but an animal, or a collection of springs which wind
each other up, without our being able to tell at what
point in this human circle, nature has begun? If
these springs differ among themselves, these differences consist only in their position and in their de-
grees of strength, and never in their nature; where-
fore the soul is but a principle of motion or a
material and sensible part of the brain, which can
be regarded, without fear of error, as the mainspring of the whole machine, having a visible influence on all the parts. The soul seems even to
have been made for the brain, so that all the other
parts of the system are but a kind of emanation
from the brain. This will appear from certain observations, made on different embryos, which I shall
now enumerate.

This oscillation, which is natural or suited to our
machine, and with which each fibre and even each
fibrous element, so to speak, seems to be endowed,
like that of a pendulum, can not keep up forever.
It must be renewed, as it loses strength, invigorated
when it is tired, and weakened when it is disturbed
by excess of strength and vigor. In this alone, true
medicine consists.

The body is but a watch, whose watchmaker is
the new chyle. Nature's first care, when the chyle

enters the blood, is to excite in it a kind of fever[74] which the chemists, who dream only of retorts, must have taken for fermentation. This fever produces a greater filtration of spirits, which mechanically animate the muscles and the heart, as if they had been sent there by order of the will.

These then are the causes or the forces of life which thus sustain for a hundred years that perpetual movement of the solids and the liquids which is as necessary to the first as to the second. But who can say whether the solids contribute more than the fluids to this movement or *vice versa*? All that we know is that the action of the former would soon cease without the help of the latter, that is, without the help of the fluids which by their onset rouse and maintain the elasticity of the blood vessels on which their own circulation depends. From this it follows that after death the natural resilience of each substance is still more or less strong according to the remnants of life which it outlives, being the last to perish. So true is it that this force of the animal parts can be preserved and strengthened by that of the circulation, but that it does not depend on the strength of the circulation, since, as we have seen, it can dispense with even the integrity of each member or organ.

I am aware that this opinion has not been relished by all scholars, and that Stahl especially had much scorn for it. This great chemist has wished to persuade us that the soul is the sole cause of all our movements. But this is to speak as a fanatic and not as a philosopher.

To destroy the hypothesis of Stahl,[75] we need not make as great an effort as I find that others have

done before me. We need only glance at a violinist.
What flexibility, what lightness in his fingers! The
movements are so quick, that it seems almost as if
there were no succession. But I pray, or rather I
challenge, the followers of Stahl who understand
so perfectly all that our soul can do, to tell me how
it could possibly execute so many motions so quickly,
motions, moreover, which take place so far from
the soul, and in so many different places. That is
to suppose that a flute player could play brilliant cadences on an infinite number of holes that he could
not know, and on which he could not even put his
finger!

But let us say with M. Hecquet[76] that all men
may not go to Corinth.[77] Why should not Stahl
have been even more favored by nature as a man
than as a chemist and a practitioner? Happy mortal,
he must have received a soul different from that
of the rest of mankind,—a sovereign soul, which,
not content with having some control over the voluntary muscles, easily held the reins of all the movements of the body, and could suspend them, calm
them, or excite them, at its pleasure! With so
despotic a mistress, in whose hands were, in a sense,
the beating of the heart, and the laws of circulation,
there could certainly be no fever, no pain, no weari-
ness,....! The soul wills, and the springs play,
contract or relax. But how did the springs of
Stahl's machine get out of order so soon? He who
has in himself so great a doctor, should be immortal.

Moreover, Stahl is not the only one who has rejected the principle of the vibration of organic
bodies. Greater minds have not used the principle

when they wished to explain the action of the heart,
....etc. One need only read the "Institutions of
Medicine" by Boerhaave[78] to see what laborious and
enticing systems this great man was obliged to in-
vent, by the labor of his mighty genius, through
failure to admit that there is so wonderful a force in
all bodies.

Willis[79] and Perrault,[80] minds of a more feeble
stamp, but careful observers of nature (whereas
nature was known to the famous Leyden professor
only through others and second hand, so to speak)
seem to have preferred to suppose a soul generally
extended over the whole body, instead of the principle which we are describing. But according to this
hypothesis (which was the hypothesis of Vergil
and of all Epicureans, an hypothesis which the
history of the polyp might seem at first sight to
favor) the movements which go on after the death
of the subject in which they inhere are due to a
remnant of soul still maintained by the parts that
contract, though, from the moment of death, these
are not excited by the blood and the spirits. Whence
it may be seen that these writers, whose solid works
easily eclipse all philosophic fables, are deceived only
in the manner of those who have endowed matter
with the faculty of thinking, I mean to say, by having expressed themselves badly in obscure and mean-
ingless terms. In truth, what is this remnant of a
soul, if it is not the "moving force" of the Leibnizians (badly rendered by such an expression),
which however Perrault in particular has really
foreseen. See his "Treatise on the Mechanism of
Animals."

Now that it is clearly proved against the Cartesians, the followers of Stahl, the Malebranchists, and the theologians who little deserve to be mentioned here, that matter is self-moved,[81] not only when organized, as in a whole heart, for example, but even when this organization has been destroyed, human curiosity would like to discover how a body, by the fact that it is originally endowed with the breath of life, finds itself adorned in consequence with the faculty of feeling, and thus with that of thought. And, heavens, what efforts have not been made by certain philosophers to manage to prove this! and what nonsense on this subject I have had the patience to read!

All that experience teaches us is that while movement persists, however slight it may be, in one or more fibres, we need only stimulate them to re-excite and animate this movement almost extinguished. This has been shown in the host of experiments with which I have undertaken to crush the systems. It is therefore certain that motion and feeling excite each other in turn, both in a whole body and in the same body when its structure is destroyed, to say nothing of certain plants which seem to exhibit the same phenomena of the union of feeling and motion.

But furthermore, how many excellent philosophers have shown that thought is but a faculty of feeling, and that the reasonable soul is but the feeling soul engaged in contemplating its ideas and in reasoning! This would be proved by the fact alone that when feeling is stifled, thought also is checked, for instance in apoplexy, in lethargy, in catalepsis, etc. For it is ridiculous to suggest that, during these stupors, the soul keeps on thinking, even though it does not remember the ideas that it has had.

As to the development of feeling and motion, it is absurd to waste time seeking for its mechanism. The nature of motion is as unknown to us as that of matter.[82]   How can we discover how it is produced unless, like the author of "The History of the Soul," we resuscitate the old and unintelligible doctrine of substantial forms? I am then quite as content not to know how inert and simple matter becomes active and highly organized, as not to be able to look at the sun without red glasses; and I am as little disquieted concerning the other incomprehensible wonders of nature, the production of feeling and of thought in a being which earlier appeared to our limited eyes as a mere clod of clay.

Grant only that organized matter is endowed with a principle of motion, which alone differentiates it from the inorganic (and can one deny this in the face of the most incontestable observation?) and that among animals, as I have sufficiently proved, everything depends upon the diversity of this organization: these admissions suffice for guessing the riddle of substances and of man. It [thus] appears that there is but one [type of organization] in the universe, and that man is the most perfect [example]. He is to the ape, and to the most intelligent animals, as the planetary pendulum of Huyghens[83] is to a watch of Julien Leroy.[84]   More instruments, more wheels and more springs were necessary to mark the movements of the planets than to mark or strike the hours; and Vaucanson,[85] who needed more skill for making his flute player

than for making his duck, would have needed still
more to make a talking man, a mechanism no longer
to be regarded as impossible, especially in the hands
of another Prometheus. In like fashion, it was
necessary that nature should use more elaborate
art in making and sustaining a machine which for
a whole century could mark all motions of the
heart and of the mind; for though one does not
tell time by the pulse, it is at least the barometer
of the warmth and the vivacity by which one may
estimate the nature of the soul. I am right! The
human body is a watch, a large watch constructed
with such skill and ingenuity, that if the wheel
which marks the seconds happens to stop, the minute
wheel turns and keeps on going its round, and in
the same way the quarter-hour wheel, and all the
others go on running when the first wheels have
stopped because rusty or, for any reason, out of
order. Is it not for a similar reason that the
stoppage of a few blood vessels is not enough to
destroy or suspend the strength of the movement
which is in the heart as in the mainspring of the
machine; since, on the contrary, the fluids whose
volume is diminished, having a shorter road to
travel, cover the ground more quickly, borne on as
by a fresh current which the energy of the heart
increases in proportion to the resistance it encoun-
ters at the ends of the blood-vessels? And is not this
the reason why the loss of sight (caused by the com-
pression of the optic nerve and by its ceasing to con-
vey the images of objects) no more hinders hearing,
than the loss of hearing (caused by obstruction of
the functions of the auditory nerve) implies the loss
of sight? In the same way, finally, does not one man

hear (except immediately after his attack) without being able to say that he hears, while another who hears nothing, but whose lingual nerves are uninjured in the brain, mechanically tells of all the dreams which pass through his mind? These phenomena do not surprise enlightened physicians at all. They know what to think about man's nature, and (more accurately to express myself in passing) of two physicians, the better one and the one who deserves more confidence is always, in my opinion, the one who is more versed in the physique or mechanism of the human body, and who, leaving aside the soul and all the anxieties which this chimera gives to fools and to ignorant men, is seriously occupied only in pure naturalism.

Therefore let the pretended M. Charp deride philosophers who have regarded animals as machines. How different is my view! I believe that Descartes would be a man in every way worthy of respect, if, born in a century that he had not been obliged to enlighten, he had known the value of experiment and observation, and the danger of cutting loose from them. But it is none the less just for me to make an authentic reparation to this great man for all the insignificant philosophers—poor jesters, and poor imitators of Locke—who instead of laughing impudently at Descartes, might better realize that without him the field of philosophy, like the field of science without Newton, might perhaps be still uncultivated.

This celebrated philosopher, it is true, was much deceived, and no one denies that. But at any rate he understood animal nature, he was the first to prove completely that animals are pure machines.[86]

And after a discovery of this importance demand-
ing so much sagacity, how can we without ingratitude fail to pardon all his errors!

In my eyes, they are all atoned for by that great
confession. For after all, although he extols the
distinctness of the two substances, this is plainly but
a trick of skill, a ruse of style, to make theologians
swallow a poison, hidden in the shade of an analogy
which strikes everybody else and which they alone
fail to notice. For it is this, this strong analogy,
which forces all scholars and wise judges to confess
that these proud and vain beings, more distinguished
by their pride than by the name of men however
much they may wish to exalt themselves, are at
bottom only animals and machines which, though
upright, go on all fours. They all have this marvelous instinct, which is developed by education
into mind, and which always has its seat in the
brain, (or for want of that when it is lacking or
hardened, in the medulla oblongata) and never in
the cerebellum; for I have often seen the cerebellum injured, and other observers* have found
it hardened, when the soul has not ceased to fulfil
its functions.

To be a machine, to feel, to think, to know how
to distinguish good from bad, as well as blue from
yellow, in a word, to be born with an intelligence
and a sure moral instinct, and to be but an animal, are therefore characters which are no more
contradictory, than to be an ape or a parrot and
to be able to give oneself pleasure.....I believe
that thought is so little incompatible with organized
matter, that it seems to be one of its properties on

* Haller in the *Transact. Philosoph.*

a par with electricity, the faculty of motion, impenetrability, extension, etc.

Do you ask for further observations? Here are some which are incontestable and which all prove that man resembles animals perfectly, in his origin as well as in all the points in which we have thought it essential to make the comparison....

Let us observe man both in and out of his shell, let us examine young embryos of four, six, eight or fifteen days with a microscope; after that time our eyes are sufficient. What do we see? The head alone; a little round egg with two black points which mark the eyes. Before that, everything is formless, and one sees only a medullary pulp, which is the brain, in which are formed first the roots of the nerves, that is, the principle of feeling, and the heart, which already within this substance has the power of beating of itself; it is the *punctum saliens* of Malpighi, which perhaps already owes a part of its excitability to the influence of the nerves. Then little by little, one sees the head lengthen from the neck, which, in dilating, forms first the thorax inside which the heart has already sunk, there to become stationary; below that is the abdomen which is divided by a partition (the diaphragm). One of these enlargements of the body forms the arms, the hands, the fingers, the nails, and the hair; the other forms the thighs, the legs, the feet, etc., which differ only in their observed situation, and which constitute the support and the balancing pole of the body. The whole process is a strange sort of growth, like that of plants. On the tops of our heads is hair in place of which the plants have leaves and flowers; everywhere is shown the same

luxury of nature, and finally the directing principle
of plants is placed where we have our soul, that
other quintessence of man.

Such is the uniformity of nature, which we are
beginning to realize; and the analogy of the animal
with the vegetable kingdom, of man with plant. Perhaps there even are animal plants, which in vege-
tating, either fight as polyps do, or perform other
functions characteristic of animals.....

We are veritable moles in the field of nature; we
achieve little more than the mole's journey and it
is our pride which prescribes limits to the limitless.
We are in the position of a watch that should say
(a writer of fables would make the watch a hero in
a silly tale): "I was never made by that fool of a
workman, I who divide time, who mark so exactly
the course of the sun, who repeat aloud the hours
which I mark! No! that is impossible!" In the
same way, we disdain, ungrateful wretches that we
are, this common mother of all kingdoms, as the
chemists say. We imagine, or rather we infer, a cause
superior to that to which we owe all, and which
truly has wrought all things in an inconceivable
fashion. No; matter contains nothing base, except
to the vulgar eyes which do not recognize her in her
most splendid works; and nature is no stupid workman. She creates millions of men, with a facility
and a pleasure more intense than the effort of a
watchmaker in making the most complicated watch.
Her power shines forth equally in creating the low-
liest insect and in creating the most highly developed
man; the animal kingdom costs her no more than the
vegetable, and the most splendid genius no more
than a blade of wheat. Let us then judge by what we

see of that which is hidden from the curiosity
of our eyes and of our investigations, and let us
not imagine anything beyond. Let us observe the
ape, the beaver, the elephant, etc., in their operations. If it is clear that these activities can not
be performed without intelligence, why refuse intelligence to these animals? And if you grant them
a soul, you are lost, you fanatics! You will in vain
say that you assert nothing about the nature of the
animal soul and that you deny its immortality. Who
does not see that this is a gratuitous assertion; who
does not see that the soul of an animal must be
either mortal or immortal, whichever ours [is], and
that it must therefore undergo the same fate as
ours, whatever that may be, and that thus [in ad-
mitting that animals have souls], you fall into Scylla
in the effort to avoid Charybdis?

Break the chain of your prejudices, arm your-
selves with the torch of experience, and you will
render to nature the honor she deserves, instead of
inferring anything to her disadvantage, from the
ignorance in which she has left you. Only open
wide your eyes, only disregard what you can not
understand, and you will see that the ploughman
whose intelligence and ideas extend no further than
the bounds of his furrow, does not differ essentially
from the greatest genius,—a truth which the dissection of Descartes's and of Newton's brains would
have proved; you will be persuaded that the imbecile and the fool are animals with human faces, as
the intelligent ape is a little man in another shape;
in short, you will learn that since everything depends
absolutely on difference of organization, a well constructed animal which has studied astronomy, can

predict an eclipse, as it can predict recovery or death when it has used its genius and its clearness of vision, for a time, in the school of Hippocrates and at the bedside of the sick. By this line of observations and truths, we come to connect the admirable power of thought with matter, without being able to see the links, because the subject of this attribute is essentially unknown to us.

Let us not say that every machine or every animal perishes altogether or assumes another form after death, for we know absolutely nothing about the subject. On the other hand, to assert that an immortal machine is a chimera or a logical fiction, is to reason as absurdly as caterpillars would reason if, seeing the cast-off skins of their fellow-caterpillars, they should bitterly deplore the fate of their species, which to them would seem to come to nothing. The soul of these insects (for each animal has his own) is too limited to comprehend the metamorphoses of nature. Never one of the most skilful among them could have imagined that it was destined to become a butterfly. It is the same with us. What more do we know of our destiny than of our origin? Let us then submit to an invincible ignorance on which our happiness depends.

He who so thinks will be wise, just, tranquil about his fate, and therefore happy. He will await death without either fear or desire, and will cherish life (hardly understanding how disgust can corrupt a heart in this place of many delights); he will be filled with reverence, gratitude, affection, and tenderness for nature, in proportion to his feeling of the benefits he has received from nature; he will be happy, in short, in feeling nature, and in being present at the enchanting spectacle of the universe, and he will surely never destroy nature either in himself or in others. More than that! Full of humanity, this man will love human character even in his enemies. Judge how he will treat others. He will pity the wicked without hating them; in his eyes, they will be but mis-made men. But in pardoning the faults of the structure of mind and body, he will none the less admire the beauties and the virtues of both. Those whom nature shall have favored will seem to him to deserve more respect than those whom she has treated in stepmotherly fashion. Thus, as we have seen, natural gifts, the source of all acquirements, gain from the lips and heart of the materialist, the homage which every other thinker unjustly refuses them. In short, the materialist, convinced, in spite of the protests of his vanity, that he is but a machine or an animal, will not maltreat his kind, for he will know too well the nature of those actions, whose humanity is always in proportion to the degree of the analogy proved above [between human beings and animals]; and following the natural law given to all animals, he will not wish to do to others what he would not wish them to do to him.

Let us then conclude boldly that man is a machine, and that in the whole universe there is but a single substance differently modified. This is no hypothesis set forth by dint of a number of postulates and assumptions; it is not the work of prejudice, nor even of my reason alone; I should have disdained a guide which I think to be so untrustworthy, had not my senses, bearing a torch, so to speak, induced me to follow reason by lighting the way themselves.

Experience has thus spoken to me in behalf of reason; and in this way I have combined the two.

But it must have been noticed that I have not allowed myself even the most vigorous and immediately deduced reasoning, except as a result of a multitude of observations which no scholar will contest; and furthermore, I recognize only scholars as judges of the conclusions which I draw from the observations; and I hereby challenge every prejudiced man who is neither anatomist, nor acquainted with the only philosophy which can here be considered, that of the human body. Against so strong and solid an oak, what could the weak reeds of theology, of metaphysics, and of the schools, avail,—childish arms, like our parlor foils, that may well afford the pleasure of fencing, but can never wound an adversary. Need I say that I refer to the empty and trivial notions, to the pitiable and trite arguments that will be urged (as long as the shadow of prejudice or of superstition remains on earth) for the supposed incompatibility of two substances which meet and move each other unceasingly? Such is my system, or rather the truth, unless I am much deceived. It is short and simple. Dispute it now who will.

THE NATURAL HISTORY OF THE SOUL.

BY

JULIEN OFFRAY DE LA METTRIE

EXTRACTS.

THE NATURAL HISTORY OF THE SOUL.

CHAPTER II. CONCERNING MATTER.

ALL philosophers who have examined attentively the nature of matter, considered in itself, independently of all the forms which constitute bodies, have discovered in this substance, diverse properties proceeding from an absolutely unknown essence. Such are, (1) the capacity of taking on different forms, which are produced in matter itself, by which matter can acquire moving force and the faculty of feeling; (2) actual extension, which these philosophers have rightly recognized as an attribute, but not as the essence, of matter.

However, there have been some, among others Descartes, who have insisted on reducing the essence of matter to simple extension, and on limiting all the properties of matter to those of extension; but this opinion has been rejected by all other modern philosophers,....so that the power of acquiring moving force, and the faculty of feeling as well as that of extension, have been from all time considered as essential properties[87] of matter.

All the diverse properties that are observed in this unknown principle demonstrate a being in which these same properties exist, a being which must therefore exist through itself. But we can not conceive, or rather it seems impossible, that a being

which exists through itself should be able neither
to create nor to annihilate itself. It is evident that
only the forms to which its essential properties
make it susceptible can be destroyed and reproduced
in turn. Thus, does experience force us to confess
that nothing can come from nothing.

All philosophers who have not known the light
of faith, have thought that this substantial principle
of bodies has existed and will exist forever, and
that the elements of matter have an indestructible
solidity which forbids the fear that the world is
going to fall to pieces. The majority of Christian
philosophers also recognize that the substantial principle of bodies exists necessarily through itself, and
that the power of beginning or ending does not
accord with its nature. One finds that this view is
upheld by an author of the last century who taught
theology in Paris.

CHAPTER III. CONCERNING THE EXTENSION OF MATTER.

Although we have no idea of the essence of matter, we can not refuse to admit the existence of the
properties which our senses discover in it.

I open my eyes, and I see around me only matter,
or the extended. Extension is then a property which
always belongs to all matter, which can belong to
matter alone, and which therefore is inseparable
from the substance of matter.

This property presupposes three dimensions in
the substance of bodies, length, width, and depth.
Truly, if we consult our knowledge, which is gained
entirely from the senses, we cannot conceive of
matter, or the substance of bodies, without having

the idea of a being which is at the same time long, broad, and deep; because the idea of these three dimensions is necessarily bound up with our idea of every magnitude or quantity.

Those philosophers who have meditated most concerning matter do not understand by the extension of this substance, a solid extension composed of distinct parts, capable of resistance. Nothing is united, nothing is divided in this extension; for there must be a force which separates to divide, and another force to unite the divided parts. But in the opinion of these physical philosophers matter has no actually active force, because every force can come only from movement, or from some impulse or tendency toward movement, and they recognize in matter, stripped of all form by abstraction, only a potential moving force.

This theory is hard to conceive, but given its principles, it is rigorously true in its consequences. It is one of those algebraic truths which is more readily believed than conceived by the mind.

The extension of matter is then but a metaphysical extension, which according to the idea of these very philosophers, presents nothing to affect our senses. They rightly think that only solid extension can make an impression on our senses. It thus seems to us that extension is an attribute which constitutes part of the metaphysical form, but we are far from thinking that extension constitutes its essence.

However, before Descartes, some of the ancients made the essence of matter consist in solid extension. But this opinion, of which all the Cartesians have made much, has at all times been victoriously combated by clear reasons, which we will set forth later, for order demands that we first examine to what the properties of extension can be reduced.

CHAPTER V. CONCERNING THE MOVING FORCE OF MATTER.

The ancients, persuaded that there is no body without a moving force, regarded the substance of bodies as composed of two primitive attributes. It was held that, through one of these attributes, this substance has the capacity for moving and, through the other, the capacity for being moved.[88] As a matter of fact, it is impossible not to conceive these two attributes in every moving body, namely, the thing which moves, and the same thing which is moved.

It has just been said that formerly the name, matter, was given to the substance of bodies, in so far as it is susceptible of being moved. When capable of moving this same matter was known by the name of "active principle"...But these two attributes seem to depend so essentially on each other that Cicero, in order better to state this essential and primitive union of matter with its moving principle, says that each is found in the other. This expresses very well the idea of the ancients.

From this it is clear that modern writers have given us but an inexact idea of matter in attempting (through a confusion ill understood) to give this name to the substance of bodies. For, once more, matter, or the passive principle of the substance of bodies, constitutes only one part of this substance. Thus it is not surprising that these modern thinkers have not discovered in matter moving force and the faculty of feeling.

It should now be evident at the first glance, it seems to me, that if there is an active principle it must have, in the unknown essence of matter, another source than extension. This proves that simple extension fails to give an adequate idea of the complete essence or metaphysical form of the substance of bodies, and that this failure is due solely to the fact that extension excludes the idea of any activity in matter. Therefore, if we demonstrate this moving principle, if we show that matter, far from being as indifferent as it is supposed to be, to movement and to rest, ought to be regarded as an active, as well as a passive substance, what resource can be left to those who have made its essence consist in extension?

The two principles of which we have just spoken, extension and moving force, are then but potentialities of the substance of bodies; for in the same way in which this substance is susceptible of movement, without actually being moved, it also has always, even when it is not moxing itself, the faculty of spontaneous motion.

The ancients have rightly noticed that this moving force acts in the substance of bodies only when the substance is manifested in certain forms; they have also observed that the different motions which it produces are all subject to these different forms or regulated by them. That is why the forms, through which the substance of bodies can not only move, but also move in different ways, were called material forms.

Once these early masters had cast their eyes on

all the phenomena of nature, they discovered in the substance of bodies, the power of self-movement. In fact, this substance either moves itself, or when it is in motion, the motion is communicated to it by another substance. But can anything be seen in this substance, save the substance itself in action; and if sometimes it seems to receive a motion that it has not, does it receive that motion from any cause other than this same kind of substance, whose parts act the one upon the other?

If, then, one infers another agent, I ask what agent, and I demand proofs of its existence. But since no one has the least idea of such an agent, it is not even a logical entity. Therefore it is clear that the ancients must have easily recognized an intrinsic force of motion within the substance of bodies, since in fact it is impossible to prove or conceive any other substance acting upon it.

Descartes, a genius made to blaze new paths and to go astray in them, supposed with some other philosophers that God is the only efficient cause of motion, and that every instant He communicates motion to all bodies. But this opinion is but an hypothesis which he tried to adjust to the light of faith; and in so doing he was no longer attempting to speak as a philosopher or to philosophers. Above all he was not addressing those who can be convinced only by the force of evidence.

The Christian Scholastics of the last centuries have felt the full force of this reflection; for this reason they have wisely limited themselves to purely philosophic knowledge concerning the motion of matter, although they might have shown that God Himself said that He had "imprinted an active principle in the elements of matter (Gen. i; Is. lxvi)."

One might here make up a long list of author-
ities, and take from the most celebrated professors
the substance of the doctrine of all the rest; but it
is clear enough, without a medley of citations, that
matter contains this moving force which animates
it, and which is the immediate cause of all the laws
of motion.

CHAPTER VI.   CONCERNING THE SENSITIVE FACULTY OF MATTER.

We have spoken of two essential attributes of
matter, upon which depend the greater number of
its properties, namely extension and moving force.
We have now but to prove a third attribute: I
mean the faculty of feeling which the philosophers
of all centuries have found in this same substance.
I say all philosophers, although I am not ignorant
of all the efforts which the Cartesians have made,
in vain, to rob matter of this faculty.   But in order
to avoid insurmountable difficulties, they have flung
themselves into a labyrinth from which they have
thought to escape by this absurd system "that animals are pure machines."[89]

An opinion so absurd has never gained admittance
among philosophers, except as the play of wit or as
a philosophical pastime.   For this reason we shall
not stop to refute it.   Experience gives us no less
proof of the faculty of feeling in animals than of
feeling in men.....

There comes up another difficulty which more
nearly concerns our vanity: namely, the impossi-
bility of our conceiving this property as a dependence or attribute of matter.   Let it not be forgotten

that this substance reveals to us only ineffable characters. Do we understand better how extension is derived from its essence, how it can be moved by a primitive force whose action is exerted without contact, and a thousand other miracles so hidden from the gaze of the most penetrating eyes, that (to paraphrase the idea of an illustrious modern writer) they reveal only the curtain which conceals them?

But might not one suppose as some have supposed, that the feeling which is observed in animated bodies, might belong to a being distinct from the matter of these bodies, to a substance of a different nature united to them? Does the light of reason allow us in good faith to admit such conjectures? We know in bodies only matter, and we observe the faculty of feeling only in bodies: on what foundation then can we erect an ideal being, disowned by all our knowledge?

However, we must admit, with the same frankness, that we are ignorant whether matter has in itself the faculty of feeling, or only the power of acquiring it by those modifications or forms to which matter is susceptible; for it is true that this faculty of feeling appears only in organic bodies.

This is then another new faculty which might exist only potentially in matter, like all the others which have been mentioned; and this was the hypothesis of the ancients, whose philosophy, full of insight and penetration, deserves to be raised above the ruins of the philosophy of the moderns. It is in vain that the latter disdain the sources too remote from them. Ancient philosophy will always hold its own among those who are worthy to judge it, because it forms (at least in relation to the subject of which I am treating) a system that is solid and well articulated like the body, whereas all these scattered members of modern philosophy form no system.

APPENDIX.

OUTLINES AND NOTES.

BY GERTRUDE CARMAN BUSSEY.

LA METTRIE'S RELATION TO HIS PRED-
ECESSORS AND TO HIS SUCCESSORS.

I. *The Historical Relation of La Mettrie to Réné Descartes* (1596-1650).

The most direct source of La Mettrie's work, if the physiological aspect of his system is set aside, is found in the philosophy of Descartes. In fact it sometimes seems as if La Mettrie's materialism grew out of his insistence on the contradictory character of the dualistic system of Descartes. He criticises Descartes's statement that the body and soul are absolutely independent, and takes great pains to show the dependence of the soul on the body. Yet though La Mettrie's system may be opposed to that of Descartes[1] from one point of view, from another point of view it seems to be a direct consequence of it. La Mettrie himself recognizes this relationship and feels that his doctrine that man is a machine, is a natural inference from Descartes's teaching that animals are mere machines.[2] Moreover La Mettrie carries on Descartes's conception of the body as a machine, and many of his detailed discussions of the machinery of the body seem to have been drawn from Descartes.

[1] "L'histoire naturelle de l'âme," chapters XI, VIII.

[2] "Man a Machine," p. 142. Cf. La Mettrie's commentary on Descartes's teaching in "Abrégé des systèmes philosophiques," *Œuvres,* Tome 2.

It should be noted that La Mettrie did justice to Descartes, and realized how much all philosophers owed to him. He insisted moreover that Descartes's errors were due to his failure to follow his own method.[3] Yet La Mettrie's method was different from that of Descartes, for La Mettrie was an empiricist[4] without rationalistic leaning. As regards doctrine: La Mettrie differed from Descartes in his opinion of matter. Since he disbelieved in any spiritual reality, he gave matter the attributes of motion and thought, while Descartes insisted that the one attribute of matter is extension.[5] It was a natural consequence of La Mettrie's disbelief in spiritual substance that he could throw doubt on the existence of God.[6] On the other hand the belief in God was one of the foundations of Descartes's system. La Mettrie tried to show that Descartes's belief in a soul and in God was merely designed to hide his true thought from the priests, and to save himself from persecution.[7]

IIa. *The Likeness of La Mettrie to the English Materialists, Thomas Hobbes* (1588-1679) *and John Toland* (1670-1721).

The influence of Descartes upon La Mettrie cannot be questioned but it is more difficult to estimate the influence upon him of materialistic philosophers.

[3] "Abrégé des systèmes, Descartes," p. 6, *Œuvres Philosophiques,* Tome 2.

[4] "Man a Machine," page 89. Cf. "L'histoire naturelle de l'âme" (or "Traité de l'âme"), *Œuvres,* 1746, p. 229.

[5] Descartes, "Principles," Part II, Prop. 4.

[6] "Man a Machine," pp. 122-126.

[7] *Ibid.,* p. 142.

Hobbes published "The Leviathan" in 1651 and "De Corpore" in 1655. Thus he wrote about a century before La Mettrie, and since the eighteenth century was one in which the influence of England upon France was very great, it is easy to suppose that La Mettrie had read Hobbes. If so, he must have gained many ideas from him. The extent of this influence is, however, unknown, for La Mettrie rarely if ever quotes from Hobbes, or attributes any of his doctrines to Hobbes.

In the first place, both Hobbes and La Mettrie are thoroughgoing materialists. They both believe that body is the only reality, and that anything spiritual is unimaginable.[8] Furthermore their conceptions of matter are very similar. According to La Mettrie, matter contains the faculty of sensation and the power of motion as well as the quality of extension.[9] This same conception of matter is held by Hobbes, for he specifically attributes extension and motion to matter, and then reduces sensation to a kind of internal motion.[10] Thus sensation also may be an attribute of matter. Moreover Hobbes and La Mettrie are in agreement on many smaller points, and La Mettrie elaborates much that is suggested in Hobbes. They both believe that the passions are dependent on bodily conditions.[11] They agree in the belief that all the differences in men are due to differences in the constitution and organi-

[8] Hobbes, "Leviathan," Part III, Chap.34; Part I, Chap. XII, Open Court Edition, p. 169.

[9] "L'histoire naturelle de l'âme," Chapters III, V, and VI.

[10] "Leviathan, Part I, Chap. I. Cf. "Concerning Body," Part IV, Chap. XXV, 2.

[11] "Man a Machine," pp. 90-91.

zation of their bodies.[12] They both discuss the nature and importance of language.[13]

Hobbes differes from La Mettrie in holding that we can be sure that God exists as the cause of this world.[14]   However even though he thinks that it is possible to know that God exists, he does not believe that we can know his nature.

La Mettrie's system may be regarded as the application of a system like that of Hobbes to the special problem of the relation of soul and body in man; for if there is nothing in the universe but matter and motion, it inevitably follows that man is merely a very complicated machine.

There is great similarity also between the doctrine of La Mettrie and that of Toland. It is interesting to note the points of resemblance and of difference.   Toland's "Letters to Serena," which contain much of his philosophical teaching, were published in 1704.   There is a possibility therefore that La Mettrie read them and gained some suggestions from them.

The point most emphasized in Toland's teaching[15] is that motion is an attribute of matter.   He argues for this belief on the ground that matter must be essentially active in order to undergo change,[16] and that the conception of the inertness of matter is based on the conception of absolute rest, and that this absolute rest is nowhere to be

---

[12] "Leviathan," Part I, Chap. VI, Molesworth Ed., p. 40. Cf. "Man a Machine," p. 90..

[13] Ibid., Part I, Chap. IV. Cf. "Man a Machine," p. 103.

[14] Ibid., Part I, Chap. XII.

[15] "Letters to Serena," V, p. 168.

[16] Ibid., p. 196.

found.[17] Since motion is essential to matter, there
is no need, Toland believes, to account for the beginning of motion. Those who have regarded matter as inert have had to find some efficient cause for
motion, and to do this, they have held that all nature
is animated. But this pretended animation is utterly
useless, since matter is itself endowed with motion.[18]
The likeness to La Mettrie is evident. La Mettrie
likewise opposes the doctrine of the animation of
matter, and the belief in any external cause of motion.[19] Yet he feels the need of postulating some
beginning of motion,[20] and although he uses the
conception so freely, he does not agree with Toland
that the nature of motion is known. He believes
that it is impossible to know the nature of motion,[21]
while Toland believes that the nature of motion is
self-evident.[22]

Another point of contrast between Toland and
La Mettrie is in their doctrines of God. Toland
believes that God, "a pure spirit or immaterial being," is necessary for his system,[23] while La Mettrie
questions God's existence and insists that immateriality and spirituality are fine words that no one
understands.

It must be admitted, in truth, that La Mettrie and
Toland have different interests and different points
of view. Toland is concerned to discover the essential nature of matter, while La Mettrie's problem

[17] *Ibid.*, p. 203.
[18] *Ibid.*, p. 199.
[19] "L'histoire naturelle de l'âme," Chap. V, p. 94.
[20] "Man a Machine," p. 139.
[21] "Man a Machine, p. 140.
[22] "Letters to Serena," V, p. 227.
[23] *Ibid.*, V, p. 234.

is to find the specific relation of body and mind. On this relation, he builds his whole system.

b. The Relation of La Mettrie to an English Sensationalist: John Locke (1632-1704).

Locke's "Essay Concerning Human Understanding" was published in 1690, and La Mettrie, like most cultured Frenchmen of the Enlightenment, was influenced by his teaching. The main agreement between Locke and La Mettrie is in their doctrine that all ideas are derived from sensation. Both vigorously oppose the belief in innate ideas,[24] teaching that even our most complex and our most abstract ideas are gained through sensation. But La Mettrie does not follow Locke in analyzing these ideas and in concluding that many sensible qualities of objects—such as colors, sounds, etc.—have no existence outside the mind.[25] He rejects Locke's doctrine of spiritual substances,[26] and opposes Locke's theistic teaching, laying stress, on the other hand, upon Locke's admission of the possibility that "thinking being may also be material."[27]

IIIa. The Likeness, probable but unacknowledged, to La Mettrie, of the French Sensationalists, Etienne Bonnot de Condillac (1715-1780) and Claude Adrien Helvetius (1715-1771).

Condillac's "Traité des sensations" was published about ten years after La Mettrie's "L'histoire na-

[24] John Locke, "Essay Concerning Human Understanding," Book I, Book II, Chap. I.

[25] Locke, "Essay," Book II, Chap. 8.

[26] Ibid., Book II, Chap. 23.

[27] Ibid., Book IV, Chap. 10. For La Mettrie's summary of Locke, cf. his "Abrégé des systèmes," Œuvres, Tome 2.

turelle de l'âme," and therefore it is probable that Condillac had read this work, and gained some ideas from it. Yet Condillac never mentions La Mettrie's name nor cites his doctrines. This omission may be accounted for by the fact that the works of La Mettrie had been so condemned that later philosophers wished to conceal the similarity of their doctrines to his. Whether the sensationalists were influenced by his teachings or not, there is such a profound likeness in their teachings, that La Mettrie may well be regarded as one of the first French sensationalists as well as one of the leading French materialists of the time.

Condillac and La Mettrie agree that experience is the source of all knowledge. As Lange suggests,[28] La Mettrie's development of reason from the imagination may have suggested to Condillac the way to develop all the faculties from the soul. La Mettrie asserts that reason is but the sensitive soul contemplating its ideas, and that imagination plays all the rôles of the soul, while Condillac elaborates the same idea, and shows in great detail how all the faculties of the soul are but modifications of sensation.[29]

Both La Mettrie and Condillac believe that there is no gulf between man and the lower animals; but this leads to a point of disagreement between the two philosophers, for Condillac absolutely denies that animals can be mere machines,[30] and we must suppose that he would the more ardently oppose the teaching that man is merely a complicated machine!

[28] F. A. Lange, "History of Materialism," Vol. II, Chap. II.

[29] "Traité des sensations," Part I.

[30] "Traité des animaux," Chap. I, p. 454.

Condillac finally, unlike La Mettrie, believes in the existence of God. A final point of contrast also concerns the theology of the two writers. La Mettrie insists that we can not be sure that there is any purpose in the world, while Condillac affirms that we can discern intelligence and design throughout the universe.[31]

Like La Mettrie and Condillac, Helvetius teaches that all the faculties of the mind can be reduced to sensation.[32] Unlike La Mettrie, he specifically distinguishes the mind from the soul, and describes the mind as a later developed product of the soul or faculty of sensation.[33] This idea may have been suggested by La Mettrie's statement that reason is a modification of sensation. Helvetius, however, unlike La Mettrie, does not clearly decide that sensation is but a result of bodily conditions, and he admits that sensation may be a modification of a spiritual substance.[34] Moreover, he claims that climate and food have no effect on the mind, and that the superiority of the understanding is not dependent on the strength of the body and its organs.[35]

La Mettrie and Helvetius resemble each other in ethical doctrine. Both make pleasure and pain the ruling motives of man's conduct. They claim that all the emotions are merely modifications of corporeal pleasure and pain, and that therefore the only principle of action in man is the desire for pleasure and the fear of pain.[36]

[31] "Traité des animaux," Chap. VI, p. 577 ff.
[32] "Treatise on Man," Sect. II, Chap. I, p. 96.
[33] *Ibid.*, Sect. II, Chap. II, p. 108.
[34] "Essays on the Mind," Essay II, Chap. I. p. 35.
[35] "Treatise on Man," Chap. XII, p. 161.
[36] *Ibid.*, Chap. IX, p. 146; Chap. VII, p. 129.

b. *The Likeness to La Mettrie of the French Materialist, Baron Paul Heinrich Dietrich von Holbach* (1723-1789).

As Condillac and Helvetius emphasize the sensa-
tionalism taught by La Mettrie, so Holbach's book
is a reiteration and elaboration of the materialism
set forth in La Mettrie's works. The teaching of
Holbach is so like that of La Mettrie, that the similarity can hardly be a coincidence.

La Mettrie regards experience as the only teacher.
Holbach dwells on this same idea, and insists that
experience is our only source of knowledge in all
matters.[37] Holbach likewise teaches that man is
a purely material being. He disbelieves in any spiritual reality whatsoever, and makes matter the only
substance in the world. He lays stress, also, on one
thought which is a natural consequence of La Mettrie's teaching. La Mettrie has limited the action
of the will and has insisted that the will is dependent
on bodily conditions. Holbach goes further and
declares repeatedly that all freedom is a delusion,
and that man is controlled in every action by rigid
necessity.[38] This teaching seems to be the natural
outcome of the belief that man is a machine.

Holbach's atheistic theology is more extreme than
his predecessor's, for La Mettrie admits that God
may exist, while Holbach vigorously opposes the
possibility. Moreover Holbach holds the opinion,
barely suggested by La Mettrie, that an atheistic
doctrine would ameliorate the condition of man-

[37] "Système de la nature," Vol. I, Chap. I, p. 6.
[38] "Système de la nature," Vol. I, Chap. VI, p. 94.

kind.[39] He insists that the idea of God has hindered the progress of reason and interfered with
natural law.   Holbach is indeed the only one of
the philosophers here discussed, who frankly adopts
a fatalistic and atheistic doctrine of the universe.
In these respects, his teaching is the culmination of
French materialism.

[39] *Ibid.*, Vol. II, Chap. XVI, p. 451, and Chap. XXVI, p. 485.
Cf. "Man a Machine," pp. 125-126.

OUTLINE OF LA METTRIE'S METAPHYS-
ICAL DOCTRINE.

[1] The references are to pages of this book.

NOTES.[1]

NOTE ON FREDERICK THE GREAT'S EULOGY.

This translation is made from the third volume, pp. 159 ff. of "Œuvres de Fréderic II., Roi de Prusse, Publiées du vivant de l'Auteur," Berlin, 1789.

La Mettrie was received at the court of Frederick the Great, when he had been driven from Holland on account of the heretical teaching of "L'Homme Machine," The "Eloge" was read by Darget, the secretary of the king, at a public meeting of the Academy of Berlin, to which, at the initiative of Frederick, La Mettrie had been admitted.

The careful reader will not fail to note that Frederick's arithmetic is at fault, and that La Mettrie died at the age of forty-one, not forty-three, years.

At a few points. perhaps, the *Eloge* demands elucidation. Coutances, like Caen, is a Norman town. St. Malo lies, just over the border, in Brittany. La Mettrie's military service was with the French in the Silesian wars against Maria Theresa. The battle of Dettingen was fought in Bavaria and was won by the Austrians through the aid given by George II of England to Maria Theresa. The battle of Fontenoy in the Netherlands was the only victory of the French in this war.

Other accounts of the life of La Mettrie are:
J. Assézat, Introduction to "L'Homme Machine," Paris, 1865.
F. A. Lange, "History of Materialism."
Ph. Damiron, "Histoire de la philosophie du dix-huitième siècle," Paris, 1858.
N. Quépat, "La philosophie matérialiste au XVIII° siècle. Essai sur La Mettrie, sa vie, et ses œuvres." Paris, 1873.

[1] Page-references are to the editions cited on pp. 205-207, except references to "Man a Machine" which are to this translation. The translated or original title of a French book is cited according as the editor has made use of translation or of French text.

NOTES ON MAN A MACHINE.

1. *"Matter may well be endowed with the faculty of thought."* Although La Mettrie attempts to "avoid this reef," by refraining from the use of these words, yet he asserts throughout his work that sensations, consciousness, and the soul itself are modifications of matter and motion.

The possibility of matter being endowed with the faculty of thought, is denied by Elie Luzac, the publisher of "L'homme machine," in his work "L'homme plus que machine." In this work he tries to disprove the conclusions of "L'homme machine." He says: "We have therefore proved by the idea of the inert state of matter, by that of motion, by that of relations, by that of activity, by that of extension, that matter can not be possessed of the faculty of thinking"...."To be brief, I say, that if, by a material substance, we understand that matter which falls under the cognizance of our senses, and which is endowed with the qualities we have mentioned, the soul can not be material: so that it must be immaterial, and, for the same reason, God could not have given the faculty of thinking to matter, since He can not perform contradictions."[1]

2. *"How can we define a being whose nature is absolutely unknown to us?"* La Mettrie uses this as an argument against the belief in a soul, and yet he later admits that the "nature of motion is as unknown to us as the nature of matter." It is difficult then to see why there is more reason to doubt the existence of spirit, than to doubt the existence of matter. Locke makes this point very well. "It is for want of reflection that we are apt to think that our senses show us nothing but material things. Every act of sensation, when duly con-

[1] "Man More than a Machine," pp. 10, 12. For statement of the editions to which these Notes make reference, see pp. 205-207.

sidered, gives us an equal view of both parts of nature, the corporeal and spiritual."[2]...."If this notion of immaterial spirit may have, perhaps, some difficulties in it not easy to be explained, we have therefore no more reason to deny or doubt the existence of such spirits, than we have to deny or doubt the existence of body because the notion of body is cumbered with some difficulties, very hard and perhaps impossible to be explained or understood by us."[3]

3. *"Author of the 'Spectacle de la nature.'"* Noel Antoine Pluche (1688-1761) was a Jansenist author. He was Director of the College of Laon, but was deprived of his position on account of his refusal to adhere to the bull "Unigenitus." Rollin then recommended him to Gasville, intendant of Normandy, who entrusted him with his son's education. He finally settled in Paris. His principal works are: "Spectacle de la nature," (Paris, 1739); "Mécanique des langues et l'art de les enseigner," (Paris, 1751); "Harmonie des Psaumes et de l'Evangile," (Paris, 1764); "Concorde de la géographie des différents ages," (Paris, 1765).[4]

La Mettrie describes Pluche in the "Essais sur l'esprit et les beaux esprits" thus: "Without wit, without taste, he is Rollin's pedant. A superficial man, he had need of the work of M. Reaumur, of whom he is only a stale and tiresome imitator in the flat little sayings scattered in his dialogues. It was with the works of Rollin as with the 'Spectacle de la Nature,' one made the fortune of the other: Gaçon praised Person, Person praised Gaçon, and the public praised them both."[5]

This quotation from La Mettrie occurs in Assézat's edition of La Mettrie's "L'homme machine," which was published as the second volume of the series "Singularités physiologiques" (1865). Assézat was a French publisher and writer. He was at one time Secretary of the Anthropological Society, and collaborated with other writers in the publication of "La Revue Nationale," "La Revue de Paris," and "La Pensée nouvelle." His notes to "L'Homme Machine" show great knowl-

[2] Locke's "Essay Concerning Human Understanding," Book II. Chap. XXIII, § 15.

[3] *Ibid.,* § 31.

[4] Condensed and translated from *La Grande Encyclopédie,* Vol. 26.

[5] Translated from a note of Assézat in "L'homme machine."

edge concerning physiological subjects. He intended to publish a complete edition of Diderot's works, but overwork on this undermined his health, so that he was unable to complete it.[6]

4. Torricelli was a physicist and mathematician who lived from 1608 to 1647. He was a disciple of Galileo, and acted as his amenuensis for three months before Galileo's death. He was then nominated as grand-ducal mathematician and professor of mathematics in the Florentine Academy. In 1643, he made his most famous discovery. He found that the height to which a liquid will rise in a closed tube, depends on the specific gravity of the liquid, and concludes from this that the column of liquid is sustained by atmospheric pressure. This discovery did away with the obscure idea of a *fuga vacui,* and laid bare the principle on which mercurial barometers are constructed. For a long time the mercurial thermometer was called the "Torricellian tube," and the vacuum which the barometer includes is still known as a "Torricellian vacuum."[7]

5. *"Only the physicians have a right to speak on this subject."* Luzac says: "'Tis true that if the materiality of the soul was proved, the knowledge of her would be an object of natural philosophy, and we might with some appearance of reason reject all arguments to the contrary which are not drawn from that science. But if the soul is not material, the investigation of its nature does not belong to natural philosophy, but to those who search into the nature of its faculties, and are called metaphysicians."[8]

6. *"Man is…a machine."* This is the first clear statement of this theory, which as the title of the work indicates, is the central doctrine of this work. Descartes had strongly denied the possibility of conceiving man as a machine. "We may easily conceive a machine to be so constructed that it emits vocables, and even that it emits some correspondent to the action upon it of external objects which cause a change in its organs,….but not that it should emit them variously so

[6] Condensed and translated from *La Grande Encyclopédie,* Vol. 4.

[7] Condensed from the *Encyclopaedia Britannica,* 9th ed., Vol. XXIII. All references are to this edition.

[8] "Man More than a Machine," p. 5.

as appositely to reply to what is said in its presence, as men of the lowest grade of intellect can do."[9]

7. *"Let us then take in our hands the staff of experience."* La Mettrie repeatedly emphasizes the belief that knowledge must come from experience. Moreover he confines this experience to sense experience, and concludes "L'histoire naturelle de l'âme" with these words: "No senses, no ideas. The fewer senses there are: the fewer ideas. No sensations experienced, no ideas. These principles are the necessary consequence of all the observations and experiences that constitute the unassailable foundation of this work."

This doctrine is opposed to the teaching of Descartes, who insists that "neither our imagination nor our senses can give us assurance of anything unless our understanding intervene "[10] Moreover Descartes believes that the senses are fallacious, and that the ideal method for philosophy is a method corresponding to that of mathematics.[11] Condillac and Holbach agree with La Mettrie's opinion. Thus, Condillac teaches that man is nothing more than what he has become by the use of his senses.[12] And Holbach says: "As soon as we take leave of experience, we fall into the chasm where our imagination leads us astray."[13]

8. "Galen (Galenus) Claudius, 130 to *circa* 210 A. D. An eminent Greek physician and philosopher. Born at Pergamus, Mysia, he studied both the Platonic and Peripatetic systems of philosophy. Satyrus instructed him in anatomy. He traveled extensively while young to perfect his education. About 165 A. D. he moved to Rome, and became very celebrated as a surgeon and practising physician, attending the family of Marcus Aurelius. He returned to Pergamus, but probably visited Rome three or four times afterwards. He wrote in philosophy, logic, and medicine. Many, probably most, of his works are lost. He was the one medical authority for thir-

[9] "Discourse on Method," Part. V.
[10] "Discourse on Method," Part IV.
[11] "Meditations," II.
[12] Traité des sensations," Part IV, Chap. IX, § 5.
[13] "Système de la nature," Vol. I, Chap. I.

teen centuries, and his services to logic and to philosophy were also great."[14]

9. The author of "L'histoire de l'âme" is La Mettrie himself.

10. Hippocrates is often termed the "father of medicine." He was born in Cos in 460 B. C. He studied medicine under his father, Heraclides, and Herodicus of Selymbria; and philosophy under Gorgias and Democritus. He was the first to separate medicine from religion and from philosophy. He insisted that diseases must be treated by the physician, as if they were governed by purely natural laws. The Greeks had such respect for dead bodies that Hippocrates could not have dissected a human body, and consequently his knowledge of its structure was limited, but he seems to have been an acute and skilful observer of conditions in the living body. He wrote several works on medicine, and in one of them showed the first principles on which the public health must be based. The details of his life are hidden by tradition, but it is certain that he was regarded with great respect and veneration by the Greeks.[15]

11. *"The different combinations of these humors...."* Compare this with Descartes's statement that the difference in men comes from the difference in the construction and position of the brain, which causes a difference in the action of the animal spirits.[16]

12. *"This drug intoxicates, like wine, coffee, etc., each in its own measure, and according to the dose."* Descartes also speaks of the effect of wine. "The vapors of wine, entering the blood quickly, go from the heart to the brain, where they are converted into spirits, which being stronger and more abundant than usual are capable of moving the body in several strange fashions."[17]

[14] Quoted from Baldwin's *Dictionary of Philosophy and Psychology,* Vol. I.

[15] Condensed from the *Encyclopaedia Britannica,* Vol. XI.

[16] "Les passions de l'âme," Part I, Art. XV, and Art. XXXIX.

[17] *Ibid.,* Part I, Art. XV.

13. The quotation from Pope is from the "Moral Essays," published 1731 to 1735, Epistle I, 1, 69.

14. Jan Baptista Van Helmont (1578-1644) was a Flemish physician and chemist. He is noted for having demonstrated the necessity of the balance in chemistry, and for having been among the first to use the word "gas." His works were published as "Ortus Medicinae," 1648.[18]

15. The author of "Lettres sur la physiognomie" was Jacques Pernety or Pernetti. He was born at Chazelle-sur-Lyon, was for some years canon at Lyons, and died there in 1777.[19]

16. Boerhaave. See Note 78.

17. Pierre Louis Moreau de Maupertuis (1698-1759) was a French mathematician, astronomer and philosopher. He supported the Newtonian theory against the Cartesians. In 1740 he became president of the Academy of Berlin. He was the head of the expedition which was sent by Louis XV to measure a degree of longitude in Lapland. Voltaire satirized Maupertuis in the "Diatribe du Docteur Akakia."[20]

18. Luzac sums up the preceding facts by saying: "Here are a great many facts, but what is it they prove? only that the faculties of the soul arise, grow, and acquire strength in proportion as the body does; so that these same faculties are weakened in the same proportion as the body is....But from all these circumstances it does not follow that the faculty of thinking is an attribute of matter, and that all depends on the manner in which our machine is made, that the faculties of the soul arise from a principle of animal life, from an innate heat or force, from an irritability of the finest parts of the body, from a subtil ethereal matter diffused through it, or in a word, from all these things taken together."[21]

19. *"The diverse states of the soul are therefore always cor-*

[18] Condensed from the *Century Dictionary*, Vol. IX.
[19] Translated and condensed from *La Grande Encyclopédie*, Vol. 26.
[20] Condensed from the *Century Dictionary*, Vol. IX.
[21] "Man More than a Machine," p. 23.

relative with those of the body." This view is in diametrical opposition to the teaching of Descartes, who says: "The soul is of a nature wholly independent of the body."[22] Yet Descartes also states that there is an intimate connection between the two. "The Reasonable Soul....could by no means be educed from the power of matter....it must be expressly created; and it is not sufficient that it be lodged in the human body, exactly like a pilot in a ship, unless perhaps to move its members, but....it is necessary for it to be joined and united more closely to the body, in order to have sensations and appetites similar to ours, and thus constitute a real man."[22]

Holbach later emphasizes this close connection between body and soul, which is so insisted upon by La Mettrie. "If freed from our prejudices we wish to see our soul, or the moving principle which acts in us, we shall remain convinced that it is part of our body, that it can not be distinguished from the body except by an abstraction, that it is but the body itself considered relatively to some of the functions or faculties to which its nature and particular organization make it susceptible. We shall see that this soul is forced to undergo the same changes as the body, that it grows and develops with the body....Finally we can not help recognizing that at some periods it shows evident signs of weakness, sickness, and death."[23]

20. "Peyronie (François Gigot de la), a French surgeon, born in Montpellier, the fifteenth of January, 1678, died the twenty-fifth of April, 1747. He was surgeon of the hospital of Saint-Eloi de Montpellier and instructor of anatomy to the Faculty; then, in 1704, served in the army. In 1717 he became reversioner of the position of first surgeon to Louis XV; in 1731, steward of the Queen's palace; in 1735, a doctor of the King; in 1736, first surgeon of the King, and chief of the surgeons of the kingdom. The greatest merit of La Peyronie is for having founded the Academy of Surgery in Paris, and for having gained special protection for surgery and surgeons in France. He wrote little."[24]

[22] "Discourse on Method," V, last paragraph.
[23] "Système de la nature," Vol. I, Chap. VII.
[24] Translated from *La Grande Encyclopédie*, Vol. 26.

21. "Willis, Thomas (1621-1675), English physician, was born at Great Bedwin, Wiltshire, on 27th January, 1621. He studied at Christ Church, Oxford; and when that city was garrisoned for the king he bore arms for the Royalists. He took the degree of bachelor of medicine in 1646, and after the surrender of the garrison applied himself to the practice of his profession. In 1660, shortly after the Restoration, he became Sedleian professor of natural philosophy in place of Dr. Joshua Cross, who was ejected, and the same year he took the degree of doctor of physic.....He was one of the first members of the Royal Society, and was elected an honorary fellow of the Royal College of Physicians in 1664. In 1666,....he removed to Westminster, on the invitation of Dr. Sheldon, Archbishop of Canterbury....He died at St. Martin's on 11th November, 1675, and was buried in Westminster Abbey."[25]

22. Fontenelle, Bernard le Bovier de. Born at Rouen, France, February 11, 1657; died at Paris, January 9, 1757. A French advocate, philosopher, poet, and miscellaneous writer. He was the nephew (through his mother) of Corneille, and was 'one of the last of the Précieux, or rather the inventor of a new combination of literature and gallantry which at first exposed him to not a little satire' (Saintsbury). He wrote 'Poésies pastorales' (1688), 'Dialogues des morts' (1683), 'Entretiens sur la pluralité des mondes' (1686), 'Histoire des oracles' (1687), 'Eloges des académiciens' (delivered 1690-1740)."[26]

23. *"In a word, would it be absolutely impossible to teach the ape a language? I do not think so."* Compare with this Haeckel's statement of the relation between man's speech and that of apes. "It is of especial interest that the speech of apes seems on physiological comparison to be a stage in the formation of articulate human speech. Among living apes there is an Indian species which is musical; the *hylobates syndactylus* sings a full octave in perfectly pure harmonious half-tones. No impartial philologist can hesitate any longer to admit that our elaborate rational language has been slowly and gradually developed out of the imperfect speech of our Pliocene simian ancestors."[27]

[25] Quoted from the *Encyclopaedia Britannica*, Vol. XXIV.
[26] Quoted from the *Century Dictionary*, Vol. IX.
[27] E. Haeckel, "The Riddle of the Universe," Chap. III.

24. Johann Conrad Amman was born at Schaffhausen, in Switzerland, in 1669. After his graduation at Basle, he practised medicine at Amsterdam. He devoted most of his attention to the instruction of deaf mutes. He taught them by attracting their attention to the motion of his lips, tongue, and larynx, while he was speaking, and by persuading them to imitate these motions. In this way, they finally learned to articulate syllables and words, and to talk. In his works "Surdus Loquens," and "Dissertatio de Loquela," he explained the mechanism of speech, and made public his method of instruction. From all accounts it seems that his success with the deaf mutes was remarkable. He died about 1730.[28]

25. " ..... the great analogy between ape and man ..... " Compare Haeckel: "Thus comparative anatomy proves to the satisfaction of every unprejudiced and critical student the significant fact that the body of man and that of the anthropoid ape are not only peculiarly similar, but they are practically one and the same in every important respect."[29]

26. Sir William Temple was born in London in 1628. He attended the Puritan College of Emmanuel, Cambridge, but left without taking his degree. After an extensive tour on the continent, he settled in Ireland in 1655. His political career began with the accession of Charles II in 1660. He is particularly noted for concluding "The Triple Alliance" between England, the United Netherlands, and Sweden, and for his part in bringing about the marriage of William and Mary, which completed the alliance of England and the Netherlands. Temple was not as successful in political work at home as abroad, for he was too honest to care to be concerned in the intrigues in English affairs, at that time. He retired from politics and died at Moor Park in 1699.

Temple wrote several works on political subjects. His "Memoirs" were begun in 1682; the first part was destroyed before it was published, the second part was published without his consent, and the third part was published by Swift after Temple's death. His fame rests more on his diplomatic work than on his writings.[30]

[28] Condensed from the *Encyclopaedia Britannica,* Vol. I.
[29] "The Riddle of the Universe," Chap. II.
[30] Condensed from the *Encyclopaedia Britannica,* Vol. XXIII.

27. "Trembley (Abraham) a Swiss naturalist, born in Geneva, the third of September, 1700, died in Geneva, the twelfth of May, 1784. He was educated in his native city, and in the Hague, where he became tutor of the son of an English resident, and later the tutor of the young duke of Richmond, with whom he traveled in Germany and Italy. In 1760, he obtained the position of librarian at Geneva, and gained a seat in the council of the 'Two Hundred.' His admirable works on the fresh-water snake procured for him his election as member of the Royal Society of London, and as correspondent of the Academy of Sciences in Paris. From 1775 to 1782 he published several works on natural religion, and articles on natural history in the 'Philosophical Transactions,' 1742-57. His most important work is 'Mémoires pour servir à l'histoire d'un genre de polype d'eau douce' (Leyden, 1744; Paris, 2 volumes)."[81]

28. *"What was man before the invention of words and the knowledge of language? An animal."* Compare this with the statement of Hobbes: "The most noble and profitable invention of all others was that of Speech, consisting of names or appellations, and their connexion,....without which there had been amongst men neither commonwealth, nor society, nor contract, nor peace, no more than amongst lions, bears, and wolves."[82]

29. Fontenelle. See note 22.

30. *"All the faculties of the soul can be correctly reduced to pure imagination."* Compare with this La Mettrie's statement in "L'histoire naturelle de l'âme": "The more one studies all the intellectual faculties, the more convinced one remains, that they are all included in the faculty of sensation, upon which they all depend so essentially that without it the soul could never perform any of its functions."[83] This resembles Condillac's doctrine of sensation: "Judgment, reflexion, desires, passions, etc., are nothing but sensation itself which is

[81] Translated from *La Grande Encyclopédie*, Vol. 31
[82] "Leviathan," Part I, Chap. IV.
[83] "L'histoire naturelle de l'âme," Chap. XIV. p. 199.

transformed in diverse ways."[84] Helvetius also says: "All the operations of the mind are reducible to sensation."[85]

31. *"See to what one is brought by the abuse of language, and by the use of those fine words (spirituality, immateriality, etc.)."* Compare Hobbes, "Though men may put together words of contradictory signification, as *spirit* and *incorporeal*; yet they can never have the imagination of anything answering to them."[86]

32. *"Man's preëminent advantage is his organism."* Luzac says: "This no more proves that organization is the chief merit of man, than that the form of a musical instrument constitutes the chief merit of the musician. In proportion to the goodness of the instrument, the musician charms by his art, and the case is the same with the soul. In proportion to the soundness of the body, the soul is in better condition to exert her faculties."[87]

33. *"Such is, I think, the generation of intelligence."* Luzac argues against this statement thus: "But if thought and all the faculties of the soul depended only on the organization as some pretend, how could the imagination draw a long chain of consequences from the objects it has embraced?"[88]

34. Pyrrhonism is "the doctrine of Pyrrho of Elis which has been transmitted chiefly by his disciple Timon. More generally, radical Scepticism in general."[89]

35. Pierre Bayle was born at Carlat in 1647. Although the child of Protestant parents, he was converted by the Jesuits. After his reconversion to Protestantism, he was driven out of France, and took refuge first in Geneva, and then in Holland. In 1675 he became professor of philosophy at the Protestant College of Sedan, and in 1681 professor of philosophy and

[84] "Traité des sensations," p. 50. Cf. *ibid.*, Chap. XII (2).

[85] "Treatise on Man," Sect. II, Chap. I, p. 4. Cf. "Essays on Mind," Essay I, Chap. I, p. 7.

[86] "Leviathan," Part I, Chap. XII.

[87] "Man More than a Machine," p. 25.

[88] *Ibid.*, p. 26.

[89] Quoted from Baldwin's *Dictionary of Philosophy*, Vol. II.

history at Rotterdam. In 1693 he was forced to resign from his position on account of his religious views.

Bayle was one of the leading French sceptics of the time. He was a Cartesian, but questioned both the certainty of one's own existence, and the knowledge derived from it. He declared that religion is contrary to the human reason, but that this fact does not necessarily destroy faith. He distinguished religion not only from science, but also from morality, and vigorously opposed those who considered a certain religion necessary for morality. He did not openly attack Christianity, yet all that he wrote awakened doubt, and his work exerted an extensive influence for scepticism.

His principal work is the "Dictionnaire historique et critique," published 1695-1697, and containing a vast amount of knowledge, expressed in a piquant and popular style. This fact made the book widely read both by scholars and by superficial readers.

36. Arnobius the Elder was born at Sicca Venerea in Numidia, in the latter part of the third century A. D. He was at first an opponent of Christianity, but was afterwards converted, and wrote "Adversus Gentes" as an apology for Christianity. In this work, he tries to answer the complaints made against Christians on the ground that the disasters of the time were due to their impiety; vindicates the divinity of Christ; and discusses the nature of the human soul. He concludes that the soul is not immortal, for he believes that the belief in the immortality of the soul would have a deteriorating influence on morality. For translation of his work compare Vol. XIX of the "Ante-Nicene Christian Library."[40]

37. *"There exists no soul or sensitive substance without remorse."* Condillac had said: "There is something in animals besides motion. They are not pure machines: they feel."[41] La Mettrie also attributed remorse to animals, but believed that they are none the less machines. Luzac said in comment: "What renders these systems completely ridiculous, is, that the persons who pronounce men machines, give them properties which belie their assertion. If beings are but machines, why do they grant a natural law, an internal sense, a kind

[40] Condensed from the *Encyclopaedia Britannica*, Vol. II.
[41] "Traité des animaux," Chap. I, p. 454.

of dread? These are ideas which can not be excited by objects which operate on our senses."[42]

38. *"Nature has created us solely to be happy."* This is a statement of the doctrine, which La Mettrie developes in his principal ethical work "Discours sur le Bonheur." He teaches that happiness rests upon bodily pleasure and pain. In "L'histoire naturelle de l'âme," La Mettrie states that all the passions can be developed from two fundamental passions, of which they are but modifications, love and hatred, or desire and aversion.[43] Like La Mettrie, Helvetius makes corporeal pleasure and pain the ruling motives for man's conduct. Thus he writes: "Pleasure and pain are and always will be the only principles of action in man."[44]...."Remorse is nothing more than a foresight of bodily pain to which some crime has exposed us."[45] He definitely makes happiness the end of human action. "The end of man is self-preservation and the attainment of a happy existence.....Man, to find happiness, should save up his pleasures, and refuse all those which might change into pains....The passions always have happiness as an object: they are legitimate and natural, and can not be called good or bad except on account of their influence on human beings. To lead men to virtue, we must show them the advantages of virtuous actions."[46] Holbach, finally, goes further than La Mettrie or Helvetius, and makes purely mechanical impulses the motives of man's action. "The passions are ways of being or modifications of the internal organs, attracted or repulsed by objects, and are consequently subject in their own way to the physical laws of attraction and repulsion."[47]

39. *"Ixions of Christianity."* Ixion, for his treachery, stricken with madness, was cast into Erebus, where he was continually scourged while bound to a fiery wheel, and forced to cry: "Benefactors should be honored."

40. *"Who can be sure that the reason for man's existence*

[42] "Man More than a Machine," p. 65.
[43] "L'histoire naturelle de l'âme," Chap. X, § XII.
[44] "Treatise on Man," Chap. X.
[45] *Ibid.,* Chap. VII.
[46] "Le vrai sens du système de la nature," Chap. IX.
[47] *Ibid.,* Vol. I, Chap. VIII, p. 140.

is not simply the fact that he exists?" Luzac opposes this by saying: "If the reason of man's existence was in man himself, this existence would be a necessary consequence of his own nature; so that his own nature would contain the cause or reason of his existence. Now since his own nature would imply the cause of his existence, it would also imply his existence itself, so that man could no more be considered as non-existent than a circle can be considered without radii or a picture without features or proportions....If the existence of man was in man himself, he would then be an invariable being."[48]

41. "Fénelon (François de Salignac de la Mothe-Fénelon), born at Château de Fénelon, Dordogne, France, August 6, 1651, died at Cambrai, France, January 7, 1715. A celebrated French prelate, orator, and author. He became preceptor of the sons of the dauphin in 1689, and was appointed archbishop of Cambrai in 1695. His works include 'Les aventures de Télémaque' (1699), 'Dialogues des morts' (1712),, Traité de l'éducation des filles' (1688), 'Explication des maximes des saints' (1697), etc. His collected works were edited by Leclère (38 vols., 1827-1830)."[49]

42. "Nieuwentyt (Bernard), a Dutch mathematician, born in Westgraafdak the tenth of August 1654, diet at Purmerend the thirtieth of May, 1718. An unrelenting Cartesian, he combated the infinitesimal calculus, and wrote a polemic against Leibnitz, concerning this subject. He wrote a theological dissertation translated into French under the title "L'existence de Dieu démontrée par les merveilles de la nature' (Paris, 1725)."[50]

43. "Abadie, James (Jacques), born at Nay, Basse-Pyrénées, probably in 1654; died at London, September 25, 1725. A noted French Protestant theologian. He went to Berlin about 1680 as minister of the French church there, and thence to England and Ireland; was for a time minister of the French church in the Savoy; and settled in Ireland as dean of Killaloe in 1699. His chief work is the 'Traité de la vérité de la reli-

[48] "Man More than a Machine," pp. 71 and 72.
[49] Quoted from the *Century Dictionary*, Vol. IX.
[50] Translated from *La Grande Encyclopédie*, Vol. 24.

gion chrétienne' (1684), with its continuation 'Traité de la divinité de nôtre Seigneur Jesus-Christ' (1689)."[51]

44. "Derham (William), English theologian and scholar, born in Stoughton, near Worcester, in 1657, died at Upminster in 1735. Pastor of Upminster in the county of Essex, he could peacefully devote himself to his taste for mechanics and natural history. Besides making studies of watch-making, and of fish, birds, and insects, published in part in the *Transactions of the Royal Society*, he wrote several works on religious philosophy. The most important, which was popular for a long time and was translated into French (1726), has as title 'Physico-Theology, or the Demonstration of the Existence and the Attributes of God, by the Works of His Creation' (1713). He wrote as complement, in 1714, his 'Astro-Theology, or the Demonstration of the Existence and Attributes of God by the Observation of the Heavens.' "[52]

45. Rais, or Cardinal de Retz (1614-1679), was a French politician and author. From his childhood he was intended for the church. He took an active part in the movement against Cardinal Mazarin, and later became cardinal, but lost his popularity, and was imprisoned at Vincennes. After escaping from there he returned to France and settled in Lorraine, where he wrote his 'Mémoires,' which tell of the court life of his time.[53]

46. Marcello Malpighi (1628-1694) was a renowned Italian anatomist and physiologist. He held the position of lecturer on medicine at Bologna in 1656, a few months later became professor at Pisa, was made professor at Bologna in 1660, went from there to Messina, though he later returned to Bologna. In 1691 he became physician to Pope Innocent XII. Malpighi is often known as the founder of microscopic anatomy. He was the first to see the marvelous spectacle of the circulation of the blood on the surface of a frog's lung. He discovered the vesicular structure of the human lung, the structure of the secreting glands, and the mucous character

[51] Quoted from the *Century Dictionary*, Vol. IX.
[52] Translated from *La Grande Encyclopédie*, Vol. 14
[53] Condensed from the *Century Dictionary*, Vol. X.

of the lower stratum of the epidermis. He was the first to undertake the finer anatomy of the brain, and he accurately described the distribution of grey matter, and of the fibre tracts in the cord. His works are: "De pulmonibus (Bologna, 1661), "Epistolae anatomicae narc. Malpighi et Car. Fracassati" (Amsterdam, 1662), "De Viscerum Structura" (London, 1669), "Anatome Plantarum" (London, 1672), "De Structura Glandularum conglobatarum" (London, 1689).[54]

47. Deism is a system of thought which arose in the latter part of the seventeenth century. Its most important representatives in England were Toland, Collins, Chubb, Shaftsbury, and Tindal. They insisted on freedom of thought and speech, and claimed that reason is superior to any authority. They denied the necessity of any supernatural revelation, and were consequently vigorously opposed by the church. Partly because of this opposition by the church, many of them argued against Christianity, and tried to show that an observance of moral laws is the only religion necessary for man. They taught that happiness is man's chief end, and that, since man is a social being, his happiness can best be gained by mutual helpfulness. Although they declared that nature is the work of a perfect being, they had a mechanical conception of the relation of God to the world, and did not, like later theists, find evidence of God's presence in all the works of nature.[55]

48. "Vanini, Lucilio, self-styled Julius Cæsar. Born at Taurisano, kingdom of Naples, about 1585; burned at the stake at Toulouse, France, February 19, 1619. An Italian free thinker, condemned to death as an atheist and magician. He studied at Rome and Padua, became a priest, traveled in Germany and the Netherlands, and began teaching at Lyons, but was obliged to flee to England, where he was arrested. After his release he returned to Lyons, and about 1617 settled at Toulouse. Here he was arrested for his opinions, condemned, and on the same day executed. His chief works are: 'Amphitheatrum aeternae Providentiae' (1615), 'De admirandis naturae reginae deaeque mortalium arcanis' (1616)."[56]

[54] Condensed from the *Encyclopaedia Britannica,* Vol. XV.
[55] Cf. A. W. Benn, "History of English Rationalism," Vol. I, Chap. III.
[56] Quoted from the *Century Dictionary,* Vol. X.

49. Desbarreaux (Jacques Vallée). A French writer, born at Paris in 1602, who died at Chalon-sur-Saône the ninth of May, 1673. He wrote a celebrated sonnet on penitence, but was rather an unbeliever and sceptic than a penitent. Guy Patin, hearing of his death, said: "He infected poor young people by his licence. His conversation was very dangerous and destructive to the public."[57]

50. Boindin (Nicolas), French scholar and author, born the twenty-ninth of May 1676 at Paris, where he died the thirtieth of November 1751. He was in the army for a while, but retired on account of ill health. He then gave himself up to literature, and wrote several plays. In 1706 he was elected Royal censor and associate of the Academy of Inscriptions. His liberty, or, as it was then called, license of mind, shut the doors of the French Academy to him, and would have caused his expulsion from the Academy of Inscriptions if he had not been so old. He died without retracting his opinions.[58]

51. Denis Diderot (1713-1784) was one of the leaders of the intellectual movement of the eighteenth century. He was at first influenced by Shaftsbury, and was enthusiastic in his support of natural religion. In his "Pensées philosophiques" (1746) he tries to show that the discoveries of natural science are the strongest proofs for the existence of God. The wonders of animal life are enough to destroy atheism for ever. Yet, while he opposes atheism, he also opposes vigorously the intolerance and bigotry of the church. He claims that many of the attributes ascribed to God are contrary to the very idea of a just and loving God.

Later, Diderot was influenced by La Mettrie and by Holbach, and became an advocate of materialism which he set forth in "Le rêve d'Alembert" and in the passages contributed to the "Système de la nature." Diderot was the editor of the "Encyclopédie."[59]

52. Trembley. See note 27.

[57] Translated and condensed from La Grande Encyclopédie, Vol. 14.

[58] Translated and condensed from La Grande Encyclopédie, Vol. 7.

[59] Condensed from F. A. Lange, "History of Materialism," Vol. II, Chap. I, and from W. Windelband, "History of Philosophy," Part V, Chap. I.

53. *"Nothing which happens, could have failed to happen."*
An enunciation of the doctrine so insisted upon by Holbach.
"The whole universe....shows us only an immense and un-
interrupted chain of cause and effect."[60]...."Necessity which
regulates all the movements of the physical world, controls
also those of the moral world."[61]

54. *"All these evidences of a creator, repeated thousands...of
times...are self-evident only to the anti-Pyrrhonians."* La Mettrie holds an opinion contrary not only to that of Descartes
and Locke, but also to that of Toland, Hobbes, and Condillac.
Descartes, for instance, says: "Thus I very clearly see that the
certitude and truth of all science depends on the knowledge
alone of the true God."[62] Hobbes asserts: "For he that from
any effect he seeth come to pass should reason to the next and
immediate cause thereof, and from thence to the cause of that
cause,....shall at last come to this, that there must be, as
even the heathen philosophers confessed, one first mover, that
is a first and an eternal cause of all things, which is that
which men mean by the name of God."[63] Toland's words are:
"All the jumbling of atoms, all the Chances you can suppose
for it, could not bring the Parts of the Universe into their
present Order, nor continue them in the same, nor cause the
Organization of a Flower or a Fly.....The Infinity of Matter
....excludes....an extended corporeal God, but not a pure
Spirit or immaterial Being."[64] Condillac writes: "A first cause,
independent, unique, infinite, eternal, omnipotent, immutable,
intelligent, free, and whose providence extends over all things:
that is the most perfect notion of God that we can form in
this life."[65] Locke declares: "From what has been said it is
plain to me we have a more certain knowledge of the existence
of a God than of anything our senses have not immediately
discovered to us. Nay I presume I may say, that we more
certainly know that there is a God, than that there is anything
else without us."[66]

[60] "Système de la nature," Vol. I, Chap. I, p. 12.
[61] *Ibid.,* Vol. II, Chap. XI,. Cf. Vol. I, Chap. VII.
[62] "Meditations," III and V.
[63] "Leviathan," Part I, Chap. XII.
[64] "Letters to Serena," V, p. 235.
[65] "Traité des animaux," Chap. VI, p. 585.
[66] "Essay Concerning Human Understanding," Book IV, Chap. X.

55. "Lucretius (Titus Lucretius Carus). Born at Rome, probably about 96 B. C., died October 15, 55 B. C. A celebrated Roman philosophical poet. He was the author of 'De rerum natura,' a didactic and philosophical poem in six books, treating of physics, of psychology, and (briefly) of ethics from the Epicurean point of view. He committed suicide probably in a fit of insanity. According to a popular but doubtless erroneous tradition, his madness was due to a love-philter administered to him by his wife."[67]

56. "Lamy (Bernard) was born in Mans in the year 1640. He studied first in the college of this city. He later went to Paris, and at Saumar studied philosophy under Charles de la Fontenelle, and theology under André Martin and Jean Leporc. He was at length called to teach philosophy in the city of Angers. He wrote a great many books on theological subjects. His philosophical works are: 'L'art de parler' (1675), 'Traité de méchanique, de l'équilibre, des solides et des liqueurs' (1679), 'Traité de la grandeur en général' (1680), 'Entretiens sur les sciences' (1684), 'Eléments de géométrie,' (1685)."[68]

57. *"The eye sees only because it is formed and placed as it is."* La Mettrie doubts whether there is any purpose in the world. Condillac, on the other hand, teaches that purpose and intelligence are shown forth in the universe. "Can we see the order of the parts of the universe, the subordination among them, and notice how so many different things compose such a permanent whole, and remain convinced that the cause of the universe is a principle without any knowledge of its effects, which without purpose, without intelligence, relates each being to particular ends, subordinated to a general end?"[69]

58. "Non nostrum inter vos tantas componere lites." Vergil, Eclogue III, line 108.

59. *"The universe will never be happy unless it is atheistic."* Although La Mettrie calls this a "strange opinion" it is clear

[67] Quoted from the *Century Dictionary,* Vol. IX.

[68] Translated and condensed from the *Dictionnaire des Sciences philosophiques,* Vol. III, Paris, 1847.

[69] "Traité des animaux," Chap. VI.

that he secretly sympathizes with it. Holbach affirms this doctrine very emphatically. "Experience teaches us that sacred opinions were the real source of the evils of human beings. Ignorance of natural causes created gods for them. Imposture made these gods terrible. This idea hindered the progress of reason."[70] "An atheist....is a man who destroys chimeras harmful to the human race, in order to lead men back to nature, to experience, and to reason, which has no need of recourse to ideal powers, to explain the operations of nature."[71]

60. *"The soul is therefore but an empty word."* Contrast this with Descartes's statement: "And certainly the idea I have of the human mind....is incomparably more distinct than the idea of any corporeal object."[72] Compare this doctrine, also, with Holbach's assertion: "Those who have distinguished the soul from the body seem to have only distinguished their brains from themselves. Truly the brain is the common center, where all the nerves spread in all parts of the human body, terminate and join together....The more experience we have, the more we are convinced that the word 'spirit' has no meaning even to those who have invented it, and can be of no use either in the physical or in the moral world."[73]

61. William Cowper (1666-1709) was an English anatomist. He was drawn into a controversy with Bidloo, the Dutch physician, by publishing under his own name Bidloo's work on the anatomy of human bodies. His principal works are: "Myotamia reformata" (London, 1694) and "Glandularum descriptio" (1702).[74]

62. William Harvey (1578-1657), an English physician and physiologist, is renowned for his discovery of the circulation of the blood. He was educated at Canterbury and Cambridge, and took his doctor's degree at Cambridge in 1602. During

---

[70] Système de la nature," Vol. II, Chap. XVI, p. 451.

[71] *Ibid.,* Chap. XXVI, p. 485. Cf. Luzac's criticism in "Man More than a Machine," p. 94.

[72] "Meditations," IV.

[73] "Système de la nature," Vol. I, Chap. VII, pp. 121-122.

[74] Condensed and translated from *La Grande Encyclopédie,* Vol. 13.

his life he held the position of Lumleian lecturer at the College of Physicians, and of physician extraordinary to James I. His principal works are: "Exercitatio de motu cordis et sanguinis" (1628), and "Exercitationes de generatione animalium" (1651).[75]

63. Francis Bacon (1551-1626) was one of the first to revolt against scholasticism and to introduce a new method into science and philosophy. He claimed that to know reality, and consequently to gain new power over reality, man must stop studying conceptions, and study matter itself. Yet he did not himself know how to gain a more accurate knowledge of nature, so that he could not put into practice the method which he himself advocated. His works are full of scholastic conceptions, though many of the implications of his system are materialistic. Lange claims,[76] indeed, that if Bacon had been more consistent and daring, he would have reached strictly materialistic conclusions. The account of the motion of the heart of the dead convict is found in "Sylva Sylvarum."[77] This book, published in 1627, a year after Bacon's death, contains the account of Bacon's experiments, and of his theories in matters of physiology, physics, chemistry, medicine, and psychology.

64. Robert Boyle, one of the greatest natural philosophers of his age, studied at Eton for three years, and then became the private pupil of the rector of Stalbridge. He traveled through France, Switzerland, and Italy, and while at Florence, studied the work of Galileo. He decided to devote his life to scientific work, and in 1645 became a member of a society of scientific men, which later grew into the Royal Society of London. His principal work was the improvement of the air-pump, and by that the discovery of the laws governing the pressure and volume of gases.

Boyle was also deeply interested in theology. He gave liberally for the work of spreading Christianity in India and America, and by his will endowed the "Boyle Lectures" to

[75] Condensed from the *Century Dictionary,* Vol. IX.

[76] F. A. Lange, "History of Materialism," Vol. I, Sec. II, Chap. III.

[77] "Sylva Sylvarum sive Historia Naturalis Latio Transcripta a J. Gruteo. Lug. Batavos, 1648. Cf. Bk. IV, Experiment 400.

demonstrate the Christian religion against atheists, theists, pagans, Jews, and Mohammedans.[78]

65. Nicolas Sténon was born at Copenhagen, 1631, and died at Schwerin in 1687. He studied at Leyden and Paris, and then settled in Florence, where he became the physician of the grand duke. In 1672 he became professor of anatomy at Florence, but three years later he gave up this posiiton and entered the church. In 1677 he was made Bishop of Heliopolis and went to Hanover, then to Munster, and finally to Schwerin. His principal work is the "Discours sur l'anatomie du cerveau" (Paris, 1669).[79]

66. La Mettrie's account of involuntary movements is much like that of Descartes. Descartes says: "If any one quickly passes his hand before our eyes as if to strike us, we shut our eyes, because the machinery of our body is so composed that the movement of this hand towards our eyes excites another movement in the brain, which controls the animal spirits in the muscles that close the eyelids."[80]

67. *"The brain has its muscles for thinking, as the legs have muscles for walking."* Neither Condillac nor Helvetius go so far. Helvetius explicitly states that it is an open question whether sensation is due to a material or to a spiritual substance.[81]

68. Giovanni Alfonso Borelli (1608-1679) was the head of the so-called iatro-mathematical sect. He tried to apply mathematics to medicine in the same way in which it had been applied to the physical sciences. He was wise enough to restrict the application of his system to the motion of the muscles, but his followers tried to extend its application and were led into many absurd conjectures. Borelli was at first professor of mathematics at Pisa, and later professor of medicine at Florence. He was connected with the revolt of Messina and was obliged to leave Florence. He retired to Rome,

[78] Condensed from the *Encyclopaedia Britannica*, Vol. IV.
[79] Translated and condensed from *La Grande Encyclopédie*, Vol. 30.
[80] "Les passions de l'âme," Part I, Art. 13.
[81] "Essays on the Mind," Essay I, Chap. I, pp. 4ff.

where he was under the protection of Christina, Queen of Sweden, and remained there until his death in 1679.[81]

69. *"For one order that the will gives, it bows a hundred times to the yoke."* Descartes, on the other hand, teaches that the soul has direct control over its voluntary actions and thoughts, and indirect control over its passions.[83] La Mettrie goes further than to limit the extent of the will, and questions whether it is ever free: "The sensations which affect us decide the soul either to will or not to will, to love or to hate these sensations according to the pleasure or the pain which they cause in us. This state of the soul thus determined by its sensations is called the will."[84] Holbach insists on this point and contends that all freedom is a delusion: "[Man's] birth depends on causes entirely outside of his power; it is without his permission that he enters this system where he has a place; and without his consent that, from the moment of his birth to the day of his death, he is continually modified by causes that influence his machine in spite of his will, modify his being, and alter his conduct. Is not the least reflexion enough to prove that the solids and fluids of which the body is composed, and that the hidden mechanism that he considers independent of external causes, are perpetually under the influence of these causes, and could not act without them? Does he not see that his temperament does not depend on himself, that his passions are the necessary consequences of his temperament, that his will and his actions are determined by these same passions, and by ideas that he has not given to himself? ....In a word, everything should convince man that during every moment of his life, he is but a passive instrument in the hands of necessity."[85]

70. The theory of animal spirits, held by Galen and elaborated by Descartes, is that the nerves are hollow tubes containing a volatile liquid, the animal spirits. The animal spirits were supposed to circulate from the periphery to the brain

[81] Condensed from the *Encyclopaedia Britannica*, Vol. IV.

[83] "Les passions de l'âme," Part I, Art. 41.

[84] "L'histoire naturelle de l'âme," Chap. XII, p. 164. Cf. Chap. XII, p. 167.

[85] "Système de la nature," Vol. I, Chap. VI, pp. 89ff.

and back again, and to perform by their action all the functions of the nerves.

71. Berkeley uses the fact that the color of objects varies, as one argument for his idealistic conclusion.[86]

72. It is hard to tell what Pythagoras himself taught, but it is certain that he taught the kinship of animals and men, and upon this kinship his rule for the abstinence from flesh was probably based. Among the writings of the later Pythagoreans we find strange rules for diet which are plainly genuine taboos. For example they are commanded "to abstain from beans, not to break bread, not to eat from a whole loaf, not to eat the heart, etc."[87]

73. Plato forbade the use of wine in his ideal republic.[88]

74. *"Nature's first care, when the chyle enters the blood, is to excite in it a kind of fever."* Thus, warmth is the first necessity for the body. Compare with this, Descartes's statement: "There is a continual warmth in our heart,....this fire is the bodily principle of all the movements of our members."[89] This is one of the many instances in which La Mettrie's account of the mechanism of the body is similar to that of Descartes.

75. "Stahl (George Ernst), born at Ansbach, Bavaria, October 21, 1660; died at Berlin, May 14, 1734. A noted German chemist, physician of the King of Prussia from 1716. His works include: 'Theoria medica vera' (1707), 'Experimenta et observationes chemicae' (1731), etc."[90]

76. Philip Hecquet (1661-1737) was a celebrated French physician. He studied at Rheims, and in 1688 became the physician of the nuns of Port Royal des Champs. He returned to Paris in 1693 and took his doctor's degree in 1697.

[86] "Dialogues Between Hylas and Philonous," I, Open Court edition; pp. 27, 28, 29. Cf. "Principles of Human Knowledge," par. 10, 15.
[87] Quoted from J. Burnet, "Early Greek Philosophy," Chap. II.
[88] Republic, III, 403.
[89] 'Les passions de l'âme," Part I, Art. VIII.
[90] Quoted from the *Century Dictionary,* Vol. X.

He was twice dean of the faculty of Paris. In 1727 he became the physician of the religious Carmelites of the suburb of Saint Jacques, and remained their physician for thirty-two years.[91]

77. The quotation: *"All men may not go to Corinth,"* is translated from Horace, Ep. 1, 19, 36. "Non cuivis homini contigit adire Corinthum."

78. Hermann Boerhaave was born at Voorhout near Leyden, on December 31, 1668. His father, who belonged to the clerical profession, destined his son for the same calling and so gave him a liberal education. At the University of Leyden, he studied under Gronovius, Ryckius and Frigland. At the death of his father, Boerhaave was left without any provision and supported himself by teaching mathematics. Vandenberg, the burgomaster of Leyden, advised him to study medicine, and he decided to devote himself to this profession. In 1693 he received his degree and began to practice medicine. In 1701 he was made "Lecturer on the Institutes of Medicine" at the University of Leyden. Thirteen years later he was appointed Rector of the University, and the same year became Professor of Practical Medicine there. He introduced into the university the system of clinical instruction. Boerhaave's merit was widely recognized, and his fame attracted many medical students from all Europe to the University of Leyden. Among these was La Mettrie whose whole philosophy was profoundly influenced by the teaching of Boerhaave. In 1728 Boerhaave was elected into the Royal Academy of Sciences of Paris, and two years later he was made a member of the Royal Society of London. In 1731 his health compelled him to resign the Rectorship at Leyden. At this time he delivered an oration, "De Honore, Medici Servitute." He died after a long illness on April 23, 1738. The city of Leyden erected a monument to him in the Church of St. Peter, and inscribed on it: "Salutifero Boerhaavii genio Sacrum."

Boerhaave was a careful and brilliant student, an inspiring teacher, and a skilful practitioner. There are remarkable accounts of his skill in discovering symptoms, and in diagnosing diseases. His chief works are: "Institutiones Medicae" (Ley-

[91] Translated and condensed from *La Grande Encyclopédie,* Vol. 19.

den, 1708); "Aphorismi de cognoscendis et curandis Morbis" (Leyden, 1709), "Libellus de Materia Medica et Remediorum Formulis" (Leyden, 1719), "Institutiones et Experimentae Chemicae" (Paris, 1724).[92]

79. Willis. (See Note 21.)

80. Claude Perrault (1613-1688) was a French physician and architect. He received his degree of doctor of medicine at Paris and practised medicine there. In 1673 he became a member of the Royal Academy of Sciences. Although he never abandoned his work in mathematics, in the natural sciences, and in medicine, he is more noted as an architect than as a physician or scientist. He was the architect of one of the colonnades of the Louvre, and of the Observatory.[93]

81. *"Matter is self-moved."* In "L'histoire naturelle de l'âme" La Mettrie claims that motion is one of the essential properties of matter. See "L'histoire naturelle de l'âme," Chap. V.

82. *"The nature of motion is as unknown to us as that of matter."* Unlike La Mettrie, Toland holds that it is possible to know the nature of matter, and declares that motion and matter can not be defined, because their nature is self-evident.[94] Holbach, resembling La Mettrie, teaches that it is futile to seek to know the ultimate nature of matter, or the cause for its existence. "Thus if any one shall ask whence matter came, we shall say that it has always existed. If any one ask, whence came movement in matter, we shall answer that for this same reason matter must have moved from eternity, since motion is a necessary consequence of its existence, its essence, and of its primitive properties, such as extent, weight, impenetrability, shape, etc.....The existence of matter is a fact; the existence of motion is another fact."[95]

83. Huyghens (Christian) was born at The Hague, 1629, and died there in 1695. He was a Dutch physicist, mathematician,

[92] Condensed from the *Encyclopaedia Britannica*, Vol. III.
[93] Translated and condensed from *La Grande Encyclopèdie*, Vol. 26.
[94] "Letters to Serena," V.
[95] "Système de la nature," Vol. II, Chap. II, p. 32.

and astronomer. He is celebrated for the invention of the pendulum clock which could measure the movements of the planets, for the improvement of the telescope, and for the development of the wave-theory of light. His principal work is "Horologium Oscillatorium" (1673).[96]

84. Julien Leroy (1686-1759) was a celebrated French watch-maker. He excelled in the construction of pendulums and of large clocks. Some have attributed the construction of the first horizontal clock to him, but this is doubtful. Among many other inventions and improvements of clocks, he invented the compensating pendulum which bears his name.[97]

85. Jacques de Vaucanson (1709-1782) was a French mechanist. From his childhood he was always interested in mechanical contrivances. In 1738 he presented to the French Academy his remarkable flute player. Soon after, he made a duck which could swim, eat, and digest, and an asp which could hiss and dart on Cleopatra's breast. He later held the position of inspector of the manufacture of silk. In 1748 he was admitted to the Academy of Sciences. His machines were left to the Queen, but she gave them to the Academy, and in the disturbances which followed the pieces were scattered and lost. Vaucanson published: "Mécanisme d'un flûteur automate" (Paris, 1738).[98]

86. "[Descartes] *understood animal nature; he was the first to prove completely that animals are pure machines.*" Contrast this with La Mettrie's former reference in "L'histoire naturelle de l'âme" to "this absurd system 'that animals are pure machines.' Such a laughable opinion," he adds, "has never gained admittance among philosophers....Experience does not prove the faculty of feeling any less in animals than in men."[99] It is evident that La Mettrie's opposition to this 'absurd system' was based upon his insistence on the similarity of men and animals. In "L'homme machine" he argues from the same premiss, that animals are machines, that men are like animals, and that therefore men also are machines.

[96] Condensed from the *Century Dictionary*, Vol. IX.
[97] Translated and condensed from *La Grande Encyclopédie*, Vol. 22.
[98] Translated and condensed from *La Grande Encyclopédie*, Vol. 31.
[99] "L'histoire naturelle de l'âme," Chap. VI.

NOTES ON THE EXTRACTS FROM "L'HISTOIRE NATURELLE DE L'AME."

87. Matter, according to La Mettrie, is endowed with extensity, the power of movement ,and the faculty of sensation. As La Mettrie says, this conception was not held by Descartes, who thought that the essential attribute of matter is exension. "The nature of body consists not in weight, hardness, color, and the like but in extension alone—in its being a substance extended in length, breadth and height."[100] Hobbes's conception of matter is very similar to that of La Mettrie. He specifically attributes motion to matter: "Motion and magnitude are the most common accidents of all bodies."[101] He does not name sensation as an attribute of matter, but he reduces sensation to motion. "Sense is some internal motion in the sentient."[102] Since motion is one of the attributes of matter, and since matter is the only reality in the universe, sensation must be attributed to matter.

88. La Mettrie always insists that matter has the power of moving itself, and resents any attempt to show that the motion is due to an outside agent. In this opinion he is in agreement with Toland. Toland says that those who have regarded matter as inert have had to find some efficient cause for motion; and to do this, they have held that all nature is animated. This pretended animation, however, is utterly useless, since matter is itself endowed with motion.

89. *"This absurd system....that animals are pure machines."* (See Note 86.)

[100] "Principles of Metaphysics," Part II, Prop. 4.
[101] "De Corpore," Part III, Chap. XV.
[102] *Ibid.*, Part IV, Chap. XXV, (2).

WORKS CONSULTED AND CITED IN THE NOTES.

(An asterisk indicates the edition to which reference is made.)

JULIEN OFFRAY DE LA METTRIE.

1745 "L'histoire naturelle de l'âme." The Hague. (This work appears as "Traité de l'âme" in La Mettrie's collected works.)

1748 "L'homme machine." Leyden.
"L'homme machine par La Mettrie, avec une introduction et des notes." J. Assézat. Paris, 1865.

1751 "Œuvres philosophiques." London (Berlin).

1764 *"Œuvres philosophiques de Monsieur de la Mettrie," Amsterdam. Besides "L'homme machine" and "Traité de l'âme," the "Œuvres philosophiques" contain the following (dates of first publication added in parentheses):
"Abrégé des systèmes."
"L'homme plante" (1748).
"Les animaux plus que machines" (1750).
"L'Anti-Sénèque" (1748).
"L'art de jouir" (1751).
"Système d'Epicure."

ELIE LUZAC.

1748 "L'homme plus que machine." London (Leyden).
*"Man More than a Machine," translated from the French of Elie Luzac, and printed with the translation of "Man a Machine" for G. Smith, 1750.

RÉNÉ DESCARTES.

1637 "Essais philosophiques," including "Discours de la méthode.
*"The Discourse on Method," translated by John Veitch. Open Court Publishing Co., 1903.

1641 "Meditationes de prima philosophia."

1644 "Principia philosophiae."
    *"The Meditations and Selections from the Principles of
      Philosophy," translated by John Veitch. Open Court
      Publishing Co., 1905.
1650 "Les passions de l'âme."
    *"Œuvres de Descartes," Vol. IV. Edited by Victor Cou-
      sin, Paris, 1824.

JOHN TOLAND.

1704 *"Letters to Serena." London. Printed for Bernard
    Lintot.

THOMAS HOBBES.

1650 "Human Nature or the Fundamental Elements of Poli-
      cie." London.
1651 "Leviathan; Or the Matter, Form, and Power of a Com-
      monwealth, Ecclesiastical & Civil." London.
1655 "Elementorum Philosophiae Sectio Prima: De Corpore."
      London.
    *English Works edited by Sir William Molesworth, 1839-
      45. Volume III. Leviathan.
    Volume IV. Human Nature.

JOHN LOCKE.

1690 "An Essay Concerning Human Understanding. London.
    *Edition of Books II and IV (with omissions) preceded
      by the English version of Le Clerc's "Eloge historique
      de feu Mr. Locke," ed. M. W. Calkins. Open Court
      Publishing Co., 1905.

ETIENNE BONNOT DE CONDILLAC.

1754 "Traité des sensations." Paris and London.
1755 "Traité des animaux." Paris and London.
    *"Œuvres completes," 23 vols. Edited by Guillaume Ar-
      noux and Mousnier. Paris, 1798. Vol. III. "Traité
      des sensations. Traité des animaux."

BARON P. H. D. VON HOLBACH.

1770 "Système de la nature," par M. Mirabaud [really Von
      Holbach].
    *Nouvelle edition avec des notes et des corrections par
      Diderot. Paris, 1821.

C. A. HELVETIUS.

1758 "De l'esprit." Paris.

*"De l'esprit, or Essays on the mind and its several faculties," translated from the French by Wiliam Mulford. London, 1810.

1772 "De l'homme, de ses facultés, et de son éducation." 2 vols. London.

*"A Treatise on Man; His Intellectual Faculties and His Education," translated from the French, with notes, by W. Hooper, M. D., 1810.

FREDERICK THE GREAT.

*"Œuvres de Frederic II., Roi de Prusse, publiées du vivant de l'auteur." Berlin, 1789: "Eloge de Julien Offray de la Mettrie," Vol. III, pp. 159 ff.

FRANCIS BACON.

*"Sylva Sylvarum, sive Historia Naturalis," transcripta a J. Grutero Lug. Batavor. 1648.

F. A. LANGE.

*"History of Materialism," translated by Ernest Chester Thomas, Boston, 1877.

W. WINDELBAND.

*"History of Philosophy," translated by J. H. Tufts, New York, 1898.

A. W. BENN.

*"History of English Rationalism in the Nineteenth Century." London, 1906.

"La Grande Encyclopédie . Inventaire Raisonné des Sciences, des Lettres, et des Arts, par une Société de Savants et de Gens de Lettres." Paris, 1885-1903.

"The Encyclopaedia Britannica. A Dictionary of Arts, Sciences, and General Literature." Ninth Edition.

"The Century Dictionary and Cyclopedia." New York.

"Dictionary of Philosophy and Psychology," edited by J. M. Baldwin. London and New York, 1901.

INDEX OF NAMES AND TITLES.

(Italicised numerals refer to pages of the French text.)